The National Conference of State Legislatures serves the legislators and staffs of the nation's 50 states, its commonwealths, and territories. NCSL was created in January 1975 from the merger of three organizations that served or represented state legislatures. NCSL is a bipartisan organization with three objectives:

- To improve the quality and effectiveness of state legislatures,
- To foster interstate communication and cooperation,
- To ensure states a strong, cohesive voice in the federal system.

The Conference has offices in Denver, Colorado, and Washington, D.C.

Reinventing the Wheel

A DESIGN FOR STUDENT ACHIEVEMENT IN THE 21ST CENTURY

By Laura L. Loyacono

National Conference of State Legislatures
William T. Pound, Executive Director

Denver Office
1560 Broadway, Suite 700
Denver, Colorado 80202

Washington Office
444 North Capitol Street, N.W., Suite 515
Washington, D.C. 20001

November 1992

Art and the encouragement of art is political in the most profound sense, not as a weapon in the struggle, but as an instrument of understanding of the futility of struggle between those who share man's faith. Aeschylus and Plato are remembered today long after the triumphs of imperial Athens are gone. Dante outlived the ambitions of 13th century Florence. Goethe stands serenely above the politics of Germany, and I am certain that after the dust of centuries has passed over our cities, we too will be remembered not for victories or defeats in battle or politics, but for our contribution to the human spirit.

John F. Kennedy

List of Tables, Figures and Photographs

The arts offer a great deal to the state and national effort to improve the performance of students and schools. It is for this reason that the National Conference of State Legislatures and the Getty Center for Education in the Arts take pride in their innovative partnership to promote new learning opportunities for children in and through the arts. This publication represents the culmination of a two-year project to study the many schools that have recognized the role that the arts play in education reform and the legislative initiatives that make these efforts possible. We are happy to present *Reinventing the Wheel: A Design for Student Achievement in the 21st Century* as a resource for state legislators and their staffs.

William T. Pound

Executive Director

National Conference of State Legislatures

Leilani Lattin Duke

Director

The Getty Center for Education in the Arts

Acknowledgements

*T*he National Conference of State Legislatures is especially grateful to the Getty Center for Education in the Arts for its generous financial support of this project and to Vicki Rosenberg, program officer, and Valsin Marmillion, president of Pacific Visions and consultant to the Getty Center, who guided it through two busy years.

The author wishes to extend special thanks to Connie Koprowicz, research analyst in NCSL's Education Program, who provided critical research and writing for the case studies. Julie Bell, also of NCSL's Education Program, helped conduct the state studies and consulted on education reform issues. Veronica O. White prepared the manuscript for typesetting, developed the charts and graphs, and reproduced copies. Barbara Starr helped with initial administrative support and data collection. Special thanks to Karen Hansen, NCSL's publications director, and Gail Loos, NCSL's marketing director, for their enthusiastic support.

To Joslyn Green, who served as the content editor, the author is forever indebted. Thanks also to Karen Fisher for serving as copy editor and proofreader. Kathy Talley-Jones, Getty Center for Education in the Arts, also reviewed the publication. Bruce Holdeman and JoRoan Lazaro at 601 Design Inc. designed the entire publication and provided the creative energy to finish this project.

The project advisers were John Myers, NCSL Education Program director; Bill Marx, fiscal analyst, House Ways and Means Committee, Minnesota; Paul Minicucci, California Joint Committee on the Arts; Len Marini, Legislative Cultural Affairs Committee, South Carolina; Sam Grabarski, Minnesota State Arts Board; Sheila Brown, Nebraska Department of Education; Steve Kaagan, art education consultant; Dean Roddenbaugh, Binny and Smith; Luke Rich, New York Senate staff; Representative Louise Miller, Washington; Senator Betty Montgomery, Ohio; Representative Peg Shreve, Wyoming; Assemblywoman Maureen Ogden, New Jersey; and MacArthur Goodwin, arts education consultant, South Carolina. The author is grateful to her numerous contacts in Oklahoma, South Carolina, Illinois, New Jersey, Minnesota, and Colorado for their help.

Thanks also to colleagues at the National Endowment for the Arts, National Assembly of State Arts Agencies, Music Educators National Conference, and Council of Chief State School Officers for valuable data and statistics.

*T*he 21st century – an era of fast-paced imagery, interconnected cultures and high technology – will be an age of challenge for our children. Including the arts (visual arts, dance, music and theater) in education provides a powerful means of engaging children in learning and improving student achievement.

As legislators and others struggle with how to improve education, we are beginning to see how the arts can play a more important role. A comprehensive arts program teaches students many skills needed to succeed in life. It helps them

- learn to solve problems and make decisions;
- build self-esteem and self discipline;
- develop informed perception;
- build skills in cooperation and group problem solving;
- develop the ability to imagine what might be;
- appreciate, understand, and be aware of different cultures and cultural values.

A growing movement by educators, arts advocates, and parents is underway promoting the arts as basic to education. They are convinced that teaching the arts to children can solve broader problems in education and help students succeed.

What lies behind this conviction? That knowledge of the arts is essential to a good education is not, after all, a new idea. Like the wheel, the idea has been around for quite a while. But in the last 10 years or so, people who care about the arts and about education have been, in effect, reinventing the wheel—adapting a familiar idea to new circumstances in a changing world.

During the past decade, at least 36 states have adopted curriculum frameworks that reflect a comprehensive approach to teaching art through programs that encompass all students, that supplement school resources with community resources (such as museums and symphonies), and that augment standard courses to meet the special needs of nontraditional students.

A comprehensive arts curriculum should teach students not only to "make art" or perform a piece of music, but to understand the meaning of works of art and their historical and social context, the artist who created them, and the basis for making informed judgments about the work. Teachers who use this comprehensive approach to teaching art—sometimes referred to as "discpline-based art education"—teach art history, art criticism, and aesthetics as well as the production of art.

Policymakers and educators alike are starting to realize that the arts are a valuable aid to learning. There is growing evidence to suggest that the arts can improve overall student achievement, help train the workforce, lower dropout rates, strengthen multi-cultural understanding, and help students with special needs. In sum, these solutions hold great promise for helping policymakers address difficult problems.

A recent report from the U.S. Department of Labor found that more than half of America's students leave school without the skills they need to find and hold good jobs. Among these skills are the ability to work with others, communication, creative thinking, self-esteem, imagination, and invention—skills that arts education helps develop. One of the strong reasons to teach the arts, then, is that they help prepare students for occupations in many fields.

In the last 20 years, arts education has made some gains in the states, as the arts are gradually being incorporated into basic education. Two factors are likely to affect the immediate future of this movement: education reform and severely strained state budgets. Education reform, now in its third "wave" since 1983, is bringing new actors, new flexibility, and new methods of assessment to education. But financial difficulties have plagued most states for the past several years. Even though arts education could contribute substantially to the success of education reform, state fiscal constraints threaten potential gains.

As education reform has swept through the states, the standards for arts education have become more rigorous and there is new emphasis on integrating the arts into education. Challenges remain, though, in areas such as preparing teachers, improving the arts curriculum and its relationship to the curriculum overall, and assessing students' progress in the arts. Arts specialists in state departments of education, their counterparts in the state arts agencies, and many others have been working hard to help school districts offer arts education.

Several states, including Minnesota, South Carolina, Oklahoma, and New Jersey have developed effective approaches to incorporating art into the basic curriculum and to assessing its effectiveness.

Improving education is never easy, especially since the central action—more students learning more—is one that a legislature can only encourage, not mandate. Improving arts education is complicated by the many different people and groups who have a part to play: the federal government, school districts, individual artists, teachers, state arts councils, museums and other cultural institutions, private foundations, and national education associations all make up the arts education "community." Collaboration between these groups has not always been the rule, but it is desirable. Legislatures can help ensure their cooperation.

As state lawmakers become deeply involved in education reform, they are assessing their proper role. Many legislators have come to the conclusion that it is time to stop micro-managing education, time instead to set broad goals for education and empower schools to meet them. This means asking what students should be able to know and do when they leave school rather than asking them to answer pre-determined questions on a standardized test. It means encouraging cooperation between arts advocates and the schools rather than dictating their every move. "This asks a lot of legislative restraint," says Representative Ken Nelson, chair of the Minnesota House Education Finance Committee. "Our challenge is to back off and let those who are closest to the students decide what's best."

A second conclusion seems just as valid: arts education is not another "special-interest" program in search of special funding, but an integral part of education. Including the arts in basic education is a way not only to keep students interested in school, but to help prepare them for college, the workplace, and ultimately to become contibuting members of society.

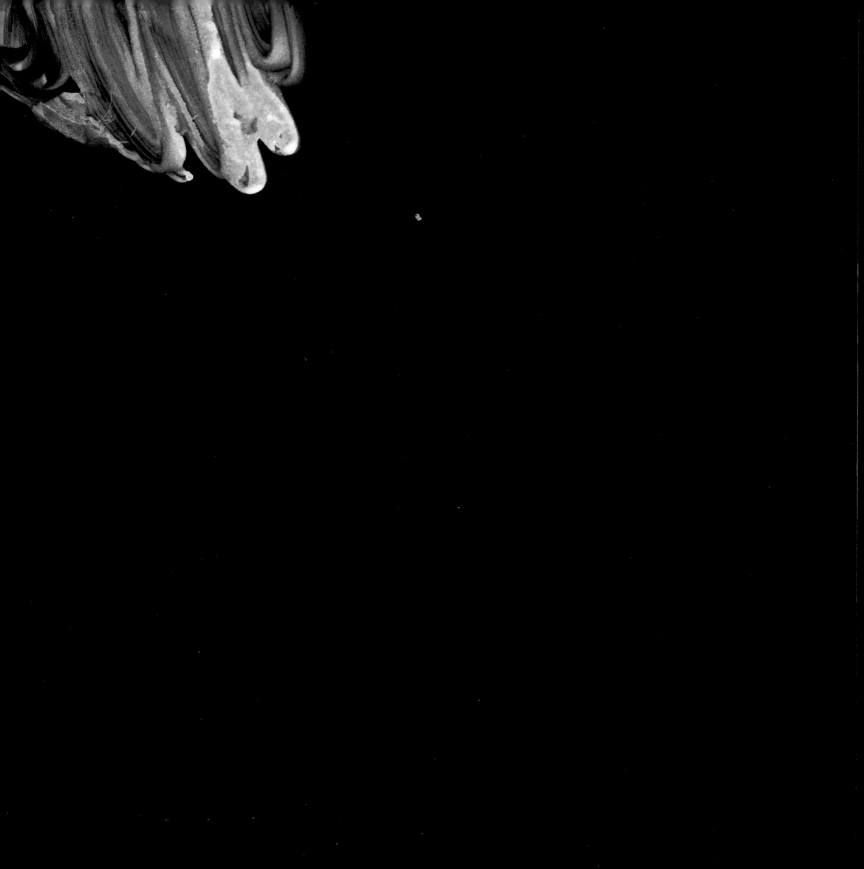

*T*he Arts and Sciences essential to the prosperity of the State and to the ornament and happiness of human life have a primary claim to the encouragement of every lover of his Country and mankind." So said George Washington, first president of the United States and one of many leaders who have recognized the importance of the arts to public and private life. From the time of the founding fathers to the present, encouragement of the arts by "every lover of his Country and mankind" has played a part in our national life.

Teaching the arts to the young has long been part of American education as well, though the motivation for teaching them has changed several times during the past two centuries. Current thinking by many education experts holds that including the arts in the basic curriculum

- excites learners and keeps them in school;
- better prepares students to achieve in the future;
- enhances critical thinking skills;
- builds multi-cultural understanding;
- provides new ways to assess student performance;
- offers a mechanism to link or integrate all subjects;
- engages traditional and nontraditional students equally.

Although we tend to think of "art" as strictly visual art, the arts considered useful to basic education include not only visual arts (painting, sculpture, photography, crafts, architecture, interior design, and graphic design), but also performing arts (dance, music, opera, musical theater, and theater), media arts (film, television, video, and radio), and literature (writing, composition, and poetry).

Another tendency has been to think that art education is only making art. But it is much more. Teaching the arts as basic to education provides new and expanded educational opportunities. Teaching all the arts to all students in a curriculum that includes the study of art history, criticism, and aesthetics, as well as art making, gives students access to important avenues of thought, understanding, and expression and prepares them to achieve at the highest level.

Even more important, arts education can help students develop skills they can transfer to other disciplines and occupations, skills like creative thinking, critical analysis, and working as part of a team. As legislators carry out their responsibility to shape American public education, they need to be aware of the role arts can play in developing good workers.

America's business leaders have begun to realize the value of the arts in education. Willard C. Butcher, chairman of the board, The Chase Manhattan Corporation, says, "I firmly believe that there is a place for the arts—music, dance, drawing, painting, writing—in the school curriculum. In the elementary grades, the arts are a valuable component in broadening a child's mind and talents. In secondary school,

"The skills needed in the 21st century are the very skills you learn through the arts—teamwork, creativity, discipline, innovation, being open to change. We are no longer a manufacturing-based economy. Part of our strength as a nation has been our creativity and innovation, precisely what we're cultivating through arts education."—Barbara Nielson, Superintendent of Education, South Carolina

the arts provide a sense of history, connecting the past to the present. When a student reaches college, a liberal arts education teaches not just clear but creative, innovative thinking. That's the kind of individual I'm interested in recruiting for Chase: one who can think conceptually, write well, and—perhaps most importantly—bring a creative outlook to the conference room table."

Public support for these ideas runs strong. According to a recent Louis Harris poll, a significant 91 percent of those polled said that it is important for schoolchildren to be exposed to the arts. Most respondents favored including art courses in the regular curriculum and paying for them out of the school budget. How important is it for children to learn about the arts? As important as learning about history and geography, said 67 percent of those polled. As important as math and science, said 60 percent; as important as learning to read and write well, said 53 percent. Respondents felt so strongly that the arts enhance learning and teach children valuable lessons for later life that they would even cut some spending on sports programs to keep the arts in school. A majority (58 percent) favored making one year of art courses a requirement for high school graduation.[1]

There has been a greater interest among national educational groups such as the Council of Chief State School Officers, the National Parent Teacher Association, and the National School Boards Association in promoting arts as basic to education. Many educators and arts advocates around the nation are convinced that teaching the arts to children can solve broader problems in education if they are taught in a comprehensive way.

What lies behind this conviction? That knowledge of the arts is essential to a good education is not, after all, a new idea. Like the wheel, the idea has been around for quite a while. But in the last 10 years or so, people who care about the arts and about education have been, in effect, reinventing the wheel—adapting a familiar idea to new circumstances in a changing world.

Teachers are finding out that the arts not only help students develop their creativity and ability to express themselves, but also improve discipline, self-esteem, and critical thinking. When study of the arts is integrated into the study of other disciplines, students learn more. Furthermore, many schools have discovered that the arts are extremely useful in teaching nontraditional students—the physically and mentally disabled, for example, and students for whom English is a second language.

Interest in including the arts in basic education has begun to surface in state legislatures. Until recently, legislators showed their support for the arts in education in other ways. Many of them have voted to include the arts in requirements for high school graduation, for example, or to fund arts "magnet" schools for gifted and talented students. Now, though, some states are experimenting with policies that make the arts a basic part of every child's education.

Taking this step requires preparation. If the arts are made basic to learning, they must, like other school subjects, be taught sequentially by teachers who are adequately trained. If more teachers are to be better trained in the arts, there will be consequences for higher education, as there will be for school districts that do not have an arts curriculum in place. Resources must be available for the arts as they are for other subjects—classroom time, administrative support, and textbooks. States and school districts must develop ways to measure student achievement in the arts.

That preparation should pay off for states, though, and handsomely. For the message of this book is that making the arts basic to education helps legislators solve broader problems in education.

The reasons to make the arts basic to education are presented in Part I, as are potential payoffs of this approach. If legislators decide to try out the new solutions described there, they face the difficulties described in Part II, difficulties that remain in the wake of many waves of incomplete education reform and which tight state budgets exacerbate.

Legislative staff should find Part III especially useful. It addresses in detail issues that have arisen in the preparation of teachers, the curriculum, and assessment. Staff and legislators in other states may wish to draw on the experience of Minnesota, New Jersey, Oklahoma, and South Carolina, whose recent efforts in arts education are also addressed in Part IV.

Part V points out where legislators who decide to strengthen arts education can find support, and it suggests that legislators are in an excellent position to bring about the collaboration on which improvements in arts education depend.

This sourcebook provides legislators and legislative staff with compelling reasons for making the arts basic to education. It demonstrates why community leaders, parents, educators and education experts alike are increasingly convinced that arts education helps prepare students to enter the 21st century.

CHAPTER ONE

DESTINATION: BETTER EDUCATION FOR ALL STUDENTS

We are all familiar with some of the reasons why the arts are included in the school curriculum. The arts help make school a more interesting and exciting place. Many a high school prides itself on the quality of the school marching band. Parents look forward to seeing their elementary school children's art projects on the walls at Back to School Night. Art has also been used to teach students about other subjects. No study of distant times or faraway places succeeds unless it gives students a sense of another society's dress, architecture, artifacts, dance, and music.

In many ways, though, the idea that the arts have much to contribute to the rest of education is newly relevant. As legislators and educators have struggled to give the arts their proper place in schools, often in the midst of controversy and uncertainty about the direction education as a whole should take, they have, as we have seen, undertaken a variety of initiatives. Many states have required students to take an arts course before they graduate from high school. Some states have set up superb schools in the performing and fine arts to serve artistically talented students. Desirable as these initiatives may be, they do not go as far as many people now think they should. The "new" idea that has won the support and enthusiasm of many experts who care about the arts is that the arts have a substantial part to play in the education for all students. The source of the experts' enthusiasm is the growing evidence that the arts strengthen the education of all students and offer special advantages for engaging students who may be difficult to reach.

Arts Education for All Students

The reasons for including the arts in education are becoming clearly understood and widely supported. Many national organizations, including the Council of Chief State School Officers, the Council for Basic Education, the National School Boards Association, and the National Conference of State Legislatures, have endorsed a more comprehensive approach to arts education.

Behind their endorsement lies an idea that Ernest L. Boyer expressed rather eloquently in *High School: A Report on Secondary Education in America*: "Art education is basic because it extends our language. It enlarges the store of images we use. It makes our understanding discriminating and comprehensive. Music, dance, and the visual arts are languages that reach all people at their deepest and most essential human level." Not surprisingly, Boyer included the arts in the core curriculum he recommended in *High School*.

Another reason to make the arts part of the core curriculum is that students who receive at least some basic training in them gain a broader educational and cultural foundation. The National Commission on Excellence in Education supported this idea in *A Nation At Risk*, which recommended that all students be taught the arts as well as English, computational and problem-solving skills, science, social studies, and foreign languages: "A high level of shared education in these basics, together with the work in the fine and performing arts and foreign languages, constitutes the mind and spirit of our culture."[1]

"The arts are a major area of human cognition, one of the ways in which we know about the world and express our knowledge. Much of what is said in the arts cannot be said in another way. To withhold artistic means of understanding is as much of a malpractice as to withhold mathematics," says Howard Gardner, Harvard Graduate School of Education.[2] In his book, *Frames of Mind: The Theory of Multiple Intelligences*, Gardner argues that seven distinct areas of competence make up human intelligence: linguistic, musical, logical/mathematical, spatial, bodily/kinesthetic, interpersonal, and intrapersonal. Since schools traditionally develop only linguistic and logical/mathematical skills, Gardner thinks they are missing an enormous opportunity to develop the whole child.

Comprehensive Arts Programs

During the past decade, at least 36 states have adopted curriculum frameworks that reflect a comprehensive approach to teaching the arts. This approach provides all students with programs that encompass all the arts, that supplement school resources with community resources, and that augment standard offerings to meet the special needs of disabled students and gifted students alike.

Comprehensive arts programs teach students many important skills needed to succeed in life. Such programs help students
· learn to solve problems and make decisions;
· build self-esteem and self-discipline;
· develop informed perception;
· build skills in cooperation and group problem solving;
· develop the ability to imagine what might be;
· appreciate, understand, and be aware of different cultures and cultural values.

History Comes Alive

At the Ashley River Creative Arts Elementary School in Charleston, South Carolina (a magnet school for students from varied ethnic and socioeconomic backgrounds), students studied state history by making pottery. By recreating Native American designs and colors on pots made of cow dung and clay, fired in a pit, they explored the symbolism that helped to shape local culture.

At the Kellogg Elementary School in Chula Vista, California, students create "living history" through the performing arts. Each year they select a different civilization to study. One year, for example they built an ancient Egyptian palace and treated guests to music and an Egyptian feast served by students wearing authentic costumes. Teachers and administrators believe this approach works better than teaching history by the book. "All students find a way to participate. . . .[O]ver the last three years. . .the number of awards for self-esteem, citizenship and academic achievement has increased," says the principal.—Charles Fowler and Bernard McMullan, Understanding How the Arts Contribute to Excellent Education.

The College Board recommends that all students study the arts, no matter what they intend to specialize in later, and that each student should undertake more intensive preparation in at least one of the art disciplines.[3]

In practice, though, schools have experienced difficulties in setting up comprehensive arts programs. Teaching the visual arts, dance, music, theater, and creative writing to all students at all levels is expensive. The strategy adopted in many school districts has been to offer some visual art and music instruction at all grade levels. However, the arts are frequently isolated rather than integrated into daily instruction. Many schools offer the arts as an extracurricular activity, forcing them to compete with sports and academic clubs.

Though many states have helped school districts expand programs and hire specialists in the various art forms, it has not been easy for schools to make their arts programs as comprehensive as they might like, especially in this time of budget shortfalls. Still, examples of successful comprehensive programs can be found in nearly every state. A few examples are provided in chapter 3.

BEP Boosts Arts Education

When North Carolina adopted its Basic Education Program (BEP) in 1984, arts education got a real boost. BEP mandated a sequential arts program for all elementary and secondary students in the state and allocated money for new teaching positions in the arts. Says Emmy Whitehead, president of the North Carolina Arts Education Association and arts coordinator for Pitt County Schools, "As school systems across the state began implementing BEP, arts education began to flourish, especially in rural areas that had never before had a sequential arts program, kindergarten through twelfth grade."

A Broader Arts Curriculum

When an arts curriculum teaches students only to make art, it is as incomplete as a literature curriculum that teaches only creative writing or a chemistry lab without a text. Many educational experts believe that if teaching the arts is to be effective it must be more content rich. Arts curricula should teach students not only to make art or perform a piece of music, but to understand the meaning of works of art, their historical and social context, the artists who created them, and the basis for making informed judgments about them.

National organizations including the Council of Chief State School Officers, The College Board, National School Boards Association, the National PTA, and the American Federation of Teachers are calling for a broader, more ambitious curriculum in the arts. The National Art Education Association, an association of professional art teachers, argues that arts education should be part of the basic K-12 curriculum, that its goals should be more ambitious than simply teaching holiday arts and crafts, and that it should reach all students.

The Getty Center for Education in the Arts has championed this comprehensive approach to teaching visual art, which is commonly referred to as discipline-based art education or DBAE. DBAE calls for the integration of ideas, skills, knowledge, and creative activity drawn from four art disciplines: art production, art criticism, art history, and aesthetics. It requires the sequential teaching of art using written curricula and instructional resources.

The national movement to teach art using the DBAE approach stems from the belief that students will have a more significant and meaningful learning experience if their education in art production, or making art, is informed by understanding the art and artifacts created by artists from around the world, questioning and interpreting works of art, and considering complex questions about the nature and meaning of art.

Through the study of
· **art production**, students learn to develop their creative abilities and express themselves through various media;
· **art history**, they learn to understand and appreciate works from different cultures, places, and times and the impact of those on artists and their works;
· **art criticism**, students learn to analyze and evaluate the structure, meaning, and significance of works of art and to make reasoned interpretations and judgments about art;
· **aesthetics**, they learn to form and articulate opinions about art and to understand the experience of art.

An expanded, comprehensive arts curriculum of the sort Getty and others support not only includes these four components but also integrates ideas, skills, knowledge, values, and creative ability from the four disciplines. Many schools are finding great success with this comprehensive approach to teaching the arts.

While the DBAE approach is most closely associated with teaching visual art, it is frequently applied to teaching the other art disciplines as well. Take music instruction. Students in a basic music class learn not only to perform a piece of music, but to analyze and evaluate music with discrimination, understand the historical and cultural backgrounds of the music, and use the vocabulary and notation of music. "The fundamental purpose of teaching music in the schools is to develop in each student, as fully as possible, the ability to perform, to create, and to understand music," says John Mahlman, executive director of the Music Educators National Conference.

Similarly, dance students not only create their own dances but discuss the history of dance forms, compare specific dance techniques (such as jazz, modern, and tap) and interpret dance meaning. "The study of dance can also provide an opportunity to learn social studies when students study the place of dance in history, in society, and in various cultures," says Judith Hanna, an educational program specialist at the U.S. Department of Education. "Without such knowledge, a dancer would not know what constitutes a

Prairie Visions

Nebraska is the home of Prairie Visions, a state consortium for discipline-based arts education. Its goal is to make understanding, appreciating, judging, and making art part of general education for all K-12 students in the state.

Initial funding for Prairie Visions came from a $625,000 matching grant from the Getty Center for Education in the Arts. As of fiscal year 1992, $1.25 million in matching funds have been provided by a consortium of arts and education organizations and private foundations including the department of education, the Woods Charitable Trust, local school districts, the Nebraska Committee for the Humanities, and the Nebraska Arts Council.

A state law mandating that music and art be provided in all elementary classrooms and offered at the secondary level supports the work of the consortium, but Nebraska is also committed to the idea of empowering school districts. "Any attempt to legislate or regulate improvement, absent local initiative, will fail," says Doug Christensen, associate commissioner, Division of Education Services. It follows that staff development is essential to Prairie Visions, which each summer conducts a statewide institute in DBAE for teachers and administrators.

In the schools, a team of teachers, the principal, and an art specialist implement the DBAE curriculum, aided by a college teacher who acts as a consultant. The program has already reached more than 1,000 teachers, administrators, and arts specialists.

unique contribution to the world of dance."[4]

Improved Overall Achievement

Policymakers and educators alike are starting to realize that the arts are a valuable aid to learning. According to New Jersey Assemblywoman Maureen Ogden, including the arts in the curriculum produces a number of direct benefits for all students. "My support for arts education isn't only about loving the arts. It's far from that, actually. Compare two similar schools, one with a strong arts curriculum and one without. You'll soon discover that there are nonartistic benefits that make the school with arts curricula a higher performance environment. Most important, in such settings the kids are excited about learning. Teachers say when the arts are used to help teach science, math, reading and the like, test scores go up in these traditional subjects."

Fifth grade teacher Rosemary Rencher of Arizona says she has found that teaching the visual arts is helpful across the curriculum, but especially during reading instruction. "If you say to students 'Can you visualize that?' now they seem to understand and be able to visualize what's being presented or discussed. I think our children had been watching so much television that they were losing the ability to create visual images for themselves inside their own heads. It's a higher level of thinking they seem to be regaining. A lost skill is coming back, and it's one that helps them learn."[5]

The reasons to teach more art in new ways are, as Assemblywoman Ogden realizes, essentially practical. There is growing evidence to suggest that solutions like those described earlier can improve overall student achievement, help train the workforce, lower dropout rates, strengthen multi-cultural education, and help students with special disabilities. In sum, the solutions hold great promise for helping policymakers address problems that have otherwise seemed intractable.

Researchers believe that students who study the arts can improve their performance in reading, writing, speaking, social studies, science, and math. One recent study by researchers from New York University found, for example, that students at the John F. Kennedy High School in the Bronx learned more history when an arts project was integrated into their history course. More students (68.7 percent) who had taken an American history course with integrated art projects passed a standardized American history test than students who took the same course with-

More Arts, Better Reading

In 1985, Principal Michael Alexander of Chicago's Guggenheim Elementary School provided staff workshops on teaching the arts across the curriculum. The reading teachers began to incorporate visual arts and drama into their lessons by asking students to draw or act out a story's main idea. After studying the body's circulatory system in a science class, students choreographed and performed a dance that represented the workings of the heart.

Principal Alexander reported a drop in teacher sick-leave days, a rise in student attendance, and improved test scores. After only one year in an arts-based curriculum, students raised their reading scores from 37 percent of the national norm to 59 percent.

"The way you understand an organism or solve a problem is by drawing it." —Louis Agassiz, renowned biologist

out art projects (54 percent).[6]

There is strong evidence that the study of music affects basic brain development. Researchers from the University of California at Irvine have found, for example, that giving young children musical training stimulates neural activity and expands their ability to think. The connection between music and mathematics is especially strong. According to a recent study by the National Arts Education Research Center, students who studied sculpture and architecture improved their understanding of geometry.[7] An Oklahoma study showed that female students raised their math scores (from a mean score of 47.85 to 80) after they participated in a visual arts program.[8] This finding is especially significant in view of recent studies showing that females typically lag in math skills.

Yet another reason to incorporate the arts into education: the interaction and creativity they encourage can nurture students' interest in learning. As one teacher put it, "Learning should be a delight—not painful." For all these reasons, there is a ground swell of support for the idea that all students, not just the gifted and talented few, should study the arts.

Corroborating evidence comes from scores on the Scholastic Aptitude Test (SAT). According to the National Center for Education Statistics, high school students who concentrate in the arts (that is, students who earn more than three credits in any combination of courses in dance, drama, design, graphic and commercial arts, crafts, fine arts, music, and creative writing) consistently score above the mean on the verbal and the math sections.

Cause and effect could be tangled here; that is, it could be argued that students who do well on the SATs are by definition bright students with wide-ranging interests or that they often come from schools that are more likely to have strong arts programs. It has also been observed, though, that SAT scores rise with the number of years students study the arts.[9]

Training the Workforce

"Can the arts possibly prepare students to enter the workforce?" "Will art help my kid get a job?" Though the legislators and parents who ask these questions may not realize it, the answer in both cases is yes. Bolstering arts education helps prepare the work force.

As *U.S. News and World Report* pointed out in a 1992 article, Japan and Germany require arts education for all students from kindergarten through high school—and "they also design the most competitive products on the world market."[10] Other leaders in product desi gn include France and Italy, where the princi-

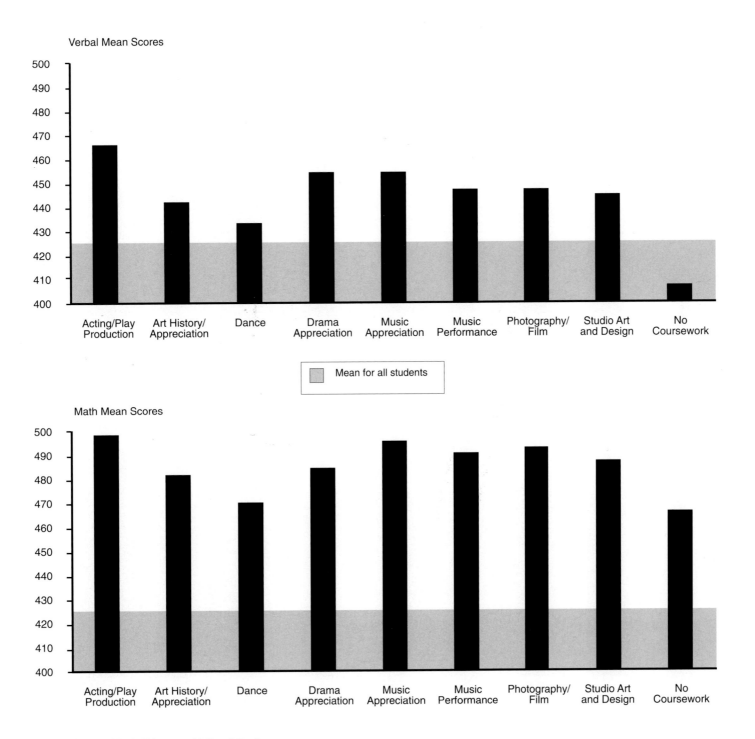

Figure 1

SAT Scores for Students Having Coursework/Exposure in Arts Education: 1989

Verbal Mean Scores

Mean for all students	

Math Mean Scores

Source: Music Educators National Conference

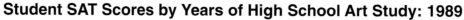

Figure 2

Student SAT Scores by Years of High School Art Study: 1989

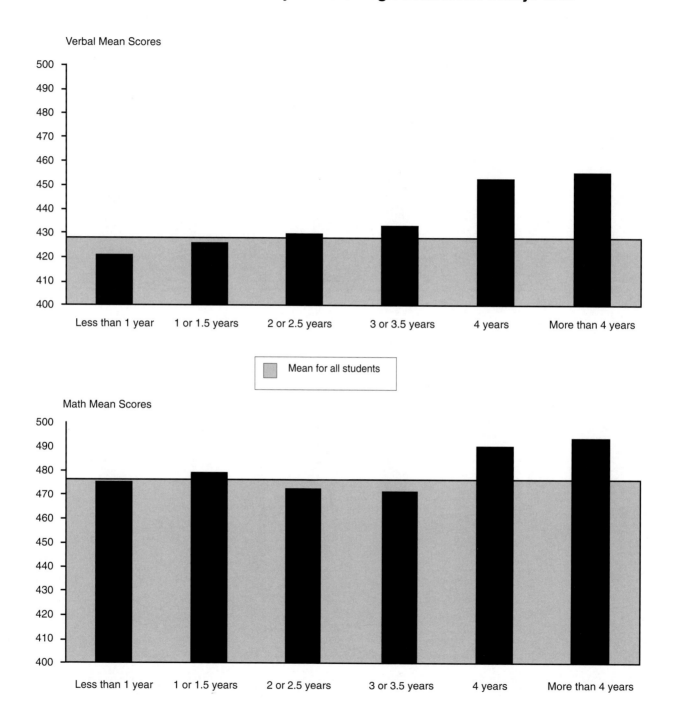

Source: Music Educators National Conference

POOR GREGOR

METAMORPHOSIS

ples of design and architecture are pivotal in the education of all children.

Though the connection between creativity and international competitiveness may have been lost in many American schools, it has not gone unnoticed by U.S. business leaders. In fact, corporate leaders have become outspoken champions of arts education. In the words of Robert E. Allen, chairman and chief executive officer, AT&T Corporation, "We live in an age increasingly ruled by science and technology, a fact that only underscores the need for more emphasis on the arts. As we find science encroaching on every field of study, we need to ensure that our humanity does not become a historical footnote. That can best be assured with a solid understanding and appreciation of the arts. A grounding in the arts will help our children to see, to bring a unique perspective to science and technology. In short, it will help them as they grow smarter to also grow wiser."

A recent report from the U.S. Department of Labor, *What Work Requires of Schools: A SCANS [Secretary's Commission on Achieving Necessary Skills] Report for America 2000,* found that more than half of America's students leave school without the skills they need to find and hold a good job. Among these skills are the ability to work with others, communication, creative thinking, self-esteem, imagination, and invention—skills that arts education helps develop. One of the strong reasons to teach the arts then, is that they help prepare students for occupations in many unrelated fields.

Another reason is that the arts are a multi-billion dollar industry. Many people in the United States work in film, television, theater, architecture, graphic design, commercial art, and music. As Canada-based researcher Harry Chartrand points out, culture is America's number-one export. "Part of the problem that the arts have in gaining recognition in the education system may be definitional," he says. "Culture is a valuable commodity that the U.S. has failed to fully recognize."

Take the theater industry. It supplies jobs not only for directors, actors, set designers, lighting technicians, and costume designers, but also for construction workers, electricians, and producers, to name but a few. Theater productions support hundreds of other jobs, not to mention the secondary economic impact that these jobs have on businesses like parking garages, hotels, and restaurants. Example: a recent two-month run of the "The Phantom of the Opera" in Denver injected more than $40 million in new dollars into the local economy.

"Out of a classroom of 30 children, maybe 10 will be employed in an arts-related occupation," says Rexford Brown, of the Education Commission of the States. "This economic factor alone is a very good reason to support the arts in education."

A Way to Keep Kids in School

New Mexico Representative Cisco McSorley is one of many people advancing the notion that the arts keep children interested in school. "In New Mexico, we are seeing progress with students who are drawn to learning in all subject areas through the arts," says McSorley. "The arts, when properly taught and integrated into the curriculum, become a vehicle for attracting students, increasing their competencies and problem-solving skills, and providing valuable experiences to kids who must go from school into the image-conscious world in which they live."

There is substantial evidence that the arts help keep students from dropping out of school. It would be an overstatement to say that they prevent a gang member or pregnant teen from dropping out. But while students are engaged in arts activities, they are exposed to other educational opportunities. South Carolina Senator Nicki Setzler, chair of the Senate Education Committee, sees arts education as a chance to reach kids who may drop out of school. "The dropout problem has been severe in South Carolina," says Setzler. "But you can reach some students through the arts, and you can help them develop higher-

Safe Haven in an Inner City

"We're in the poorest congressional district in the nation" was the unfortunate claim to fame of the St. Augustine School of the Arts, which is located in an area often termed a "war zone": the South Bronx, New York. Underenrollment nearly closed the school in 1986. But then came a transformation and a new claim to fame. St. Augustine changed from a traditional school to a performing arts school where the principal hires and fires teachers, and teachers and parents help develop the curriculum.

Though St. Augustine specializes in the performing arts, admission is based on need, not auditions. Families pay $900 yearly tuition, $2,000 less than the actual cost per student and $4,000 less than the average cost in New York public schools. Academic and disciplinary standards are rigorous. To arts education St. Augustine adds instruction in career opportunities, grooming habits, timeliness, and self-motivation.

Enrollment has soared, and 98 percent of the students now meet state academic standards, a far cry from neighboring schools where fewer than half the students can read at grade level.—Judith Hanna, "Using the Arts As a Dropout Prevention Tool," *Brown University Child Behavior and Development Letter*, March 1991.

order thinking skills."

According to Judith Hanna, U.S. Department of Education, using music, mime, and dance to enact historical events in the social studies curriculum attracts and holds the attention of many youngsters where traditional teaching methods would not. "This is basic, for if a student does not give attention to a subject, event, or idea, learning cannot take place," says Hanna.[11]

Like many a legislator, Robert McMullen, who teaches social studies in Littleton, Colo., says he's "always looking for more money for basic things." But, he adds, "I've seen many students who don't like those subjects do well in the arts. It's where they thrive. Without the arts they would turn away from school."

A Key to Multi-Cultural Understanding

Many policymakers and educators are concerned that education has been ineffective in serving minority students. With the existence of approximately 276 different ethnic groups in the United States—170 of which are Native Americans[12]—an increasing demand has been placed upon the schools. Hispanic, African-American, Asian, and Native American students make up a growing percentage of students in the public schools; by the year 2000 one in three students will be from an ethnic or national minority group.[13] Unfortunately, minorities tend to make up the majority of economically disadvantaged students.

Yet teaching methods have generally not changed to accommodate these students' needs.

Because dance, painting, and music all transcend language barriers, the arts have long served to bring societies together. Partly for these reasons, no other school subject is more attuned to cultural diversity than the arts. Arts education provides students with ways to express themselves. The arts help develop nonverbal skills such as perception, imagination, and creativity and also verbal skills such as vocabulary, metaphorical language, and critical thinking. So it is not surprising that schools of various ethnic composition are experimenting with the arts to reach students—or that the experiments are succeeding.

• The Holbrook school district in Arizona serves an isolated, economically depressed area with a student population that is approximately 52 percent Native American. In the elementary grades, art is taught exclusively by general classroom teachers, all of whom have attended comprehensive arts work-

"Through using the visual arts, I've been able to reach children I couldn't reach doing anything else. It's a way of winning them over to their own articulate selves."—Toni Ann Gomez, first grade teacher in a bilingual classroom, Montebello Unified School District, California

shops over the last three years. The Holbrook art program is multi-cultural. It focuses on Native American art, especially Navajo art, but at the same time is designed to broaden the perspective of Native American students by using artists and art from outside their culture.

• In Kansas City, Mo., the school district and community organizations are using dance to combat a rising dropout rate. Through the Kansas City Friends of Alvin Ailey Camp program, African-American students are learning about their heritage from dance and the music that accompanies it. Ailey Camp uses dance education to promote literacy and prevent at-risk children from dropping out. Program organizers believe that the excitement generated through dance education can have a synergistic effect—that students' enjoyment of moving rhythmically can be used to stimulate their interest in learning other subjects like English and social studies.

• A study of 200 southern high schools found that the arts contributed to desegregation, positive self-esteem, and academic achievement. There tended to be more cross-racial interaction in performing and visual arts classes than in other classes, and male students in schools with an additional arts teacher scored 5 percent to 10 percent higher on measures of self-esteem and academic achievement.[14]

From examples like these and preliminary research, it seems that arts education holds considerable promise for strengthening multi-cultural education.

Help for Nontraditional Students

Many schools use the arts as a way to reach students with special needs, particularly students with learning and developmental disabilities and other at-risk students. The theory—and it has been borne out in the experience of a growing number of teachers—is that the arts provide a crucial link to education success. The arts offer students with disabilities productive ways to connect with themselves and their environment.

According to many teachers, dance improves motor skills and the ability to follow directions. In schools in Washington, D.C., for example, a dance troupe founded by the late Alvin Ailey has helped mentally and physically challenged students strengthen their perceptual awareness, enhance their self-image, and increase their flexibility and strength.

"Active learning experiences in the arts process can engage the child's interest, lengthen his or her attention span and on-task behavior, and increase aesthetic awareness and imagination to respond, interact, express, create, and enjoy a fuller life," says William Freeman, executive director, Accessible Arts, Inc.

The New Visions Dance Project is an effort to assist blind students through the arts. Started in the Queens School for Career Development and the Jessie Isador Strauss School in New York, the project is sponsored by Very Special Arts, a national organization dedicated to enriching the lives of people with disabilities. By attending dance workshops, blind students learn to improve their independent-living skills.

The New Visions program has had broad appeal. Alabama, Florida, Michigan, and other

states have adopted it, and in Iowa the program has expanded to include students with mental retardation, developmental disabilities, and hearing impairment. In Wisconsin, Very Special Arts Wisconsin and the Wisconsin Department of Instruction help school districts bring students with disabilities into the classroom with other children. The department distributes federal Public Law 94-142 funds (Model Cities Project) to districts so they can incorporate the arts into the individual education plans of all children with disabilities.

"The proof is in watching the kids develop," according to New York Senator Nick Spano, chair of the Senate Mental Hygiene Committee and proponent of the Very Special Arts Training Center. An outspoken critic of the school system's inability to serve the handicapped, Spano calls for methods to serve the "forgotten populations." "When they create sculpture or a painting, they have such an obvious sense of accomplishment. Just watching them makes it all worthwhile," says Spano.

The visual arts have also proved useful in reaching nontraditional students. The school district in Portland, Ore., is one of many in which DBAE art education is infused into classes in English as a second language, classes for students with severe learning disabilities, and other special classes. According to Faith Clover, Portland's PK-5 art curriculum specialist, art provides a language for these students: "For many it is a crucial link between observation and verbal skills—they can connect with visual images and use them."[15]

New thinking about the arts in education and a growing body of experience in schools across the nation strongly suggest that the arts are not "frills," but instead a very useful—though still underused—tool for improving education overall. Current views differ from earlier calls for teaching more art in schools in at least two important ways. The rallying cry is not "art for art's sake," but, as New Jersey Assemblywoman Maureen Ogden has said, art for the sake of "educational benefits" to all students. A second significant shift has been to the idea that arts education works best when it is integrated with the rest of education rather than an intermittent experience for only some students.

Both concepts merit consideration by state legislators who often hear why education reform is not working and are often asked to fund special programs. The promise that new methods of art education hold is that they DO work—and they work when art is NOT a special program but instead basic to education.

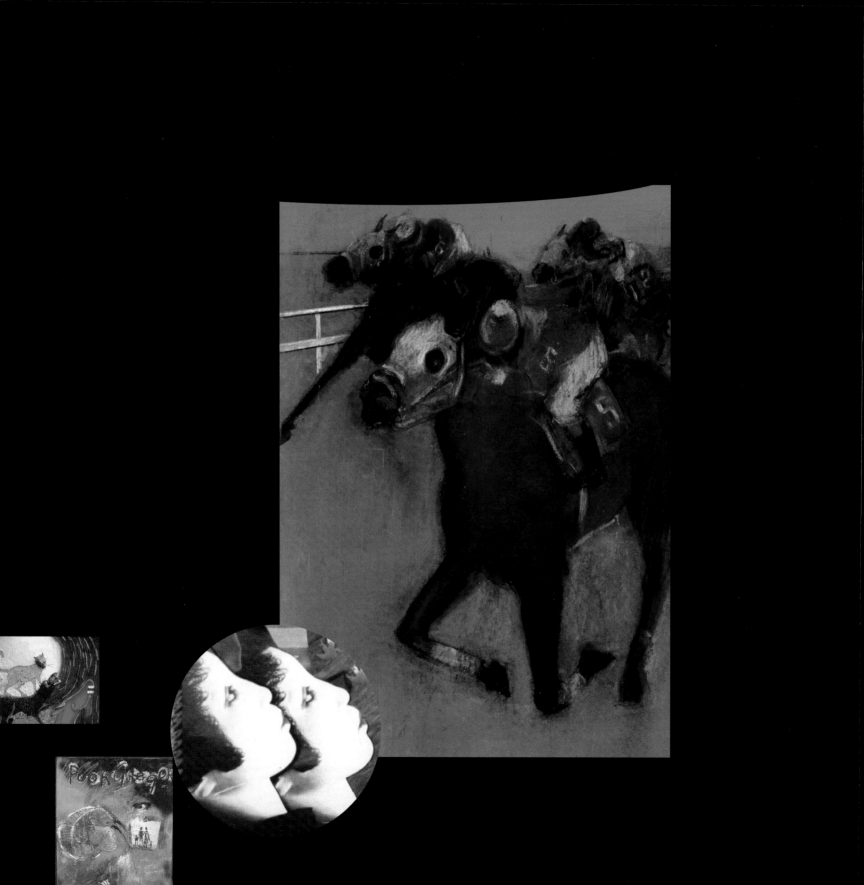

CHAPTER TWO

OBSTACLES IN THE ROAD

In the last 20 years, arts education has made some gains in the states, as the arts are gradually being incorporated into basic education. But its future is far from clear.

Two factors are likely to affect the immediate future: education reform and severely strained state budgets. Education reform, now in its third "wave" since 1983, is bringing new actors, new flexibility, and new methods of assessment to education. But financial difficulties have plagued most states for the past several years. Even though arts education could prosper with education reform and contribute substantially to its success, state fiscal constraints may cancel out potential gains.

This chapter summarizes trends in state education reform and state economies and looks at how these trends are affecting the arts and arts education. All the news is not grim: there are indications that arts education can emerge from a difficult period to serve broad educational purposes for all students.

Education Reform

The road to education reform seems very long. Theories about how to improve education have regularly come and gone for nearly a decade, yet students still do not appear to be learning more and better overall. Many schools have become experimental laboratories for new methods, new ideas, and new philosophies about teaching and learning. Yet, after all this, we are left with little concrete evidence about what works.

The first wave of education reform was set in motion in 1983 by the release of *A Nation at Risk*. This report, prepared under the leadership of Terrell Bell, who was then secretary of education, warned that inadequacies in American education endangered our standing in a competitive global economy and likened the situation to an "act of war" by a hostile power. Most states responded to his call for reform by improving measurable standards. They set stricter graduation requirements, raised teachers' salaries, and instituted minimum competency tests for teachers and students.

By the end of the 1980s, it seemed clear that these reforms were not having the desired effect. What reliable measures we had of student achievement showed little or no improvement. Despite an infusion of effort and money, the academic performance of most students remained stagnant.

According to many observers, the first wave of reform was inadequate because rigid responses by states and school districts failed to recognize the wide variety of school conditions and student needs. The early reforms were "top-down," that is, states attempted to mandate change through the centralized bureaucracy of state education agencies. The theory of top-down management was that schools should comply with a standard set of regulations, administered by the superintendent or school board and devised to affect all schools in a relatively similar manner.

By contrast, the second wave of education reform has emphasized decentralization. It is based on a "bottom-up" philosophy that recognizes the virtue of allowing each school to base education policy on its own circumstances. The result has been a movement toward "site-based management." The theory that the best approach to improving education rests with the people most directly affected—with principals, teachers, students, and parents—has led, for example, to the use of local school councils to govern schools. Also popular has been the use of alternative methods to assess what students are learning, such as assessing progress through portfolios rather than simply relying on standardized test scores.

The effectiveness of education reforms is always difficult to evaluate. Some of the most quantifiable measures—standardized test scores, attendance/dropout rates, grade-point averages—have not proved to be reliable indicators of achievement. Furthermore, it is difficult to attribute changes in these and other indicators to a single reform. In addition, the second wave of reform has not been in effect long enough to evaluate. Clearly, though, a philosophy of teaching and learning that emphasizes differences in students and schools has important implications for arts education because the arts have always emphasized differences rather than similarities, always fostered creativity in learning rather than memorization and standard answers.

Meanwhile, a third wave of education reform is bringing new actors into education policymaking. In announcing national goals and the "America 2000" strategy, the president and governors have assumed leadership roles in framing the objectives of education reform. Their actions ensure that the performance of American education will be near the top of the national policy agenda for several years. Education is no longer strictly a local concern.

This most recent wave of reform may have some negative effects on arts education, however. The national goals emphasize science and mathematics, for example, and make no mention of the role of the arts in a "world-class curriculum." Arts educators around the country have mounted campaigns to convey the message that the arts are crucial to achieving the president's education strategy.

Their message apparently has been heard. On June 4, 1992, Education Secretary Lamar Alexander unveiled the America 2000 Arts Partnership sponsored jointly by the U.S. Department of Education, the National Endowment for the Arts, and the National Endowment for the Humanities. The development of "world-class" standards in the arts is the centerpiece of the partnership, called National Standards for Education in the Arts project.

Straine Budgets

Funding for education, including arts education, is contingent on the economic health of states and local governments. In the past, the arts have had to compete for limited funds, and the outlook for the future is no brighter. States face escalating costs in a number of key areas—skyrocketing health care costs, mandates from courts to improve prison conditions, rising welfare costs, and infrastructure needs—which are putting severe pressure on their budgets. If the arts traditionally fare best in prosperous times, the immediate outlook is bleak.

Education enjoyed significant increases in state funding during the latter half of the 1980s as the school improvement craze swept the nation and states enjoyed a period of relative prosperity. Another reason for the increases was the success of court cases challenging the equity of state funding mechanisms. In response to court pressure, Kentucky, New Jersey, and Oklahoma passed major tax increases to boost education funding. School finance lawsuits are still pending in 22 states.

But fiscal conditions in the states deteriorated seriously in FY 1991 and 1992. According to NCSL's annual survey of the states, nearly three-quarters of the states had revenue shortfalls in FY 1991. Nearly half the states had to cut FY 1992 budgets in the middle of the year to meet balanced-budget requirements.

Education has traditionally been the largest item in state budgets, and in FY 1992 it still accounted for an average of 50 percent of all general-fund spending. But as state fiscal conditions deteriorated, education began to feel the strain. In FY 1991, spending for K-12 education rose only 3.8 percent, barely covering inflation and down significantly from the 10 percent increase in FY 1990. For FY 1992, states budgeted an increase of 8.9 percent. This number is deceiving, however; some states deferred funding from the previous year, while others have cut below appropriated levels. Complicating the picture is the growth in enrollments in key states like California and Florida, where expenditures per pupil are falling even as overall funding for education rises.[1]

In constant 1990-91 dollars, total public school K-12 expenditures decreased from $5,748 per pupil in 1990-91 to $5,702 in 1991-92.[2] State appropriations for higher education, which had been rising each year for at least three decades, fell in real terms between FY 1991 and FY 1992, by a total of $72 million.[3]

The slow growth of revenues has combined with escalating costs to create severe problems. Tax increases in FY 1991 and FY 1992 are the largest back-to-back increases on record, both in nominal dollars and as a percentage of state budgets. Further increases—for education or other programs—risk a voter backlash like the one that occurred in New Jersey. In 1991, Missouri voters rejected (by nearly a 2-1 margin) a sales and income tax increase that the legislature had approved to increase state aid to education. Oklahoma voters rejected an attempt to roll back the education tax increase approved by the Legislature in 1990, but they have since approved a measure that will require a two-thirds vote in the Legislature for future increases.

Although K-12 education has escaped the budget ax so far, little new money is likely. Some states may turn to lotteries or other earmarked revenue sources to fund education. These sources do not produce much money, however, and states tend to offset earmarked funds by reducing general-fund appropriations.

The implication: Education reform will have to focus on how to do things better at current spending levels. It is here that the arts can make a significant contribution.

Taking the Case for the Arts to Court

Charging that the state has failed to provide an adequate education for its children, the American Civil Liberties Union and 26 Louisiana school districts have filed two lawsuits. The suits, which are supported by music educators, math teachers, and parents, charge in part that recent budget cuts for arts education have left Louisiana schools "arts-impoverished."

This action was inspired by a 1989 suit against the state of Kentucky where the state supreme court decided that all Kentucky high school graduates need "sufficient grounding in the arts to enable each student to appreciate his or her cultural and historic heritage."—Miriam Horn, *U.S. News and World Report*, March 30, 1992

The Arts in Education Reform

Even though education reform has focused on the higher-order skills that the arts help students develop, most reforms so far have not acknowledged the contribution the arts can make. The failure of the president and the governors to acknowledge the arts in their national goals is only one example.

At least partially responsible for this lack of recognition may be the traditional view of arts education as a sort of second-class citizen. It is argued that arts education is not central to academic training, that it is not a rigorous discipline, that it does not help prepare students for the workforce, and that society offers other ways for people to learn about the arts. These views have been widely challenged. But the prevalence of the traditional view offers significant political challenges to arts supporters.

Developments during the second wave of reform pose some problems for arts education. Although the purpose of site-based management is to promote qualities like those that arts education promotes in students—independent thought, creativity, flexibility, and so forth—the effects of decentralized decision-making on arts education may not always be benign. The local school councils, sometimes referred to as "collaborative decision-making teams," or CDMs, generally, are responsible for curriculum, personnel, and budget decisions, though they vary in size, representation, and authority. Since the purpose of site-based management is to give schools flexibility, any curriculum change is fair game. If a CDM decides to eliminate arts education or music classes, it usually can. Arts education advocates from several school districts that are experimenting with site-based management report that the arts are suffering as a result.

The power that parents and community representatives are gaining over curriculum has interesting implications, since these people bring different perspectives to curriculum decisions than teachers and principals. Will non-educators find arts education desirable—or frivolous? So far, there are indications that, assuming they must choose between computers and musical instruments, CDMs will pick computers.

Funding the Arts on a Shoestring

Perhaps because the arts are frequently seen as frills rather than as an essential part of education, spending on arts education is small — an estimated 6 percent of secondary and elementary budgets. In many school districts, the situation is even more grim, as arts education becomes a casualty of budget cuts.

A further source of financial strain is the fact that many states have increased graduation requirements in arts education since the 1980s. In some cases, states have mandated higher requirements but failed to supply money to meet them. In Texas, for example, the Legislature in 1982 required that all public school students receive comprehensive arts education (prekindergarten through grade 12), but provided no funding. The state department of education provides some assistance, but, in general, school districts are expected to pay for the new plan.

Higher Test Scores Mean More Money

In South Carolina, the Aiken Grammar School has integrated creative writing, visual arts, dance, music, drama, and media arts into the general curriculum. Students scores on the Stanford Achievement Test and the California Test of Basic Skills have risen so markedly that the U.S. Department of Education named Aiken a National Blue Ribbon School of Excellence. This national award has in turn encouraged the legislature to allocate more money for arts education.

It is not clear what effect funding alone has on arts education. Nor is it clear precisely how much money is spent on arts education.

Some spending relates directly to arts education—such as expenditures for art supplies, musical instruments, classroom space, and teacher training. But spending on, for example, field trips to museums, the symphony, or zoos is more difficult to isolate. Many states and districts have integrated arts into general education so completely that the funding is not singled out by subject area. Other states spend large amounts of money on specialized schools for the arts but do little to support the arts in general education.

As a 1990 NCSL survey revealed, states generally include money for arts education in the budget for the department of education; arts education does not show up as a separate line item in the education budget. Other budgetary arrangements vary by state.

· In many states, such as Arizona and Colorado, school districts allocate state funds at their own discretion.

· Like many other states, Alabama reports that the state department of education does not spend any money specifically on arts education, except for $25,000 from a tax check-off program.

· California appropriates "seed money" for 10 sites under the Specialized High School Funding bill, Chapter 6 of 1982 SB 813. Currently, $200,000 per year is allocated for this project, which serves both art and science education programs.

· Delaware gave school districts $6.5 million in 1990 for 66 visual arts teachers and 89 music teachers.

· In Florida, the Legislature appropriates $250,000 per year to the state department of education for arts education research, in-service training, and curriculum development. School districts pay for support personnel, supplies and equipment, textbooks, field trips, and special projects.

· The Hawaii Legislature allocates money ($218,000 in FY 92-93) for the Artists in Schools program. The program includes all art disciplines and serves all schools in the state.

· Kansas appropriates $94,000 (FY 93) to the department of education to support the Accessible Arts program housed within the Kansas School for the Blind.

· In South Carolina, the legislature appropriates 1.2 million annually (FY 92 and 93) to fund pilot projects in school districts.

Federal Money

The only federal money for arts education comes to state arts agencies through the National Endowment for the Arts, generally with the requirement that the state agencies find matching funds. (No federal money for arts education comes to education agencies.) According to the NEA, every state receives grants for arts education.

Once the arts agencies match the funds, they distribute grants to schools, arts institutions, and cultural agencies. On average, arts education, which is often a line item in the agency's budget, receives about 14 percent of the grant funds. Some states help their arts agencies use federal funds. The Illinois legislature, for example, appropriates $500,000 a year to the Illinois Arts Council for a summer school for the arts, artists-in-residence programs, and other federal matching-grant programs.

Sometimes state school boards allocate federal money from other sources to arts education, such as money from Compensatory Education (Chapter 1) and Education Consolidation and Improvement Act (Chapter 2) education block grants. Kentucky, for example, appropriates Chapter 2 funds to special arts programs. Colorado has used Chapter 2 funds to support an arts specialist at the department of education. Wisconsin uses federal funds to support Very Special Arts, a program to provide arts education to children and adults with disabilities.

Long-T Funding

Funds for "special initiatives" or funds reserved for field trips to museums are often the first to be cut by the districts. But if the arts are to be a meaningful component of education, arts education needs consistent, long-term funding and support. Strategies for long-term support are beginning to surface in a number of states. In some instances, arts agencies are initiating pilot projects with federal support, then using that support to leverage long-term state commitments. Arts groups and departments of education are forming partnerships to leverage money from the legislatures and from the private sector. Arizona has dedicated a portion of the state corporate tax filing fee to arts education, and Utah is considering dedicating a portion of the two-cent user fee on video rentals for arts education.

Finding long-term money is made more difficult by the overall poor financial condition of states, which has inclined legislatures to reduce or even eliminate money for arts councils. This situation has been aggravated by conservative religious organizations that are calling for the abolishment of arts councils, on the grounds that the arts are "anti-Christian."

State support for arts councils fell 22 percent in FY 1992. In Michigan, where the governor proposed eliminating the council, the budget has been reduced from $13 million to $5 million. In the last four years, Massachusetts has cut its arts council budget from $27 million (FY 1989) to $3.6 million (FY 1992). Cuts like these undoubtedly send a message to schools that the arts are expendable.

Arts education clearly faces challenges in the 1990s. But very real opportunities could lie ahead. It is true that education reform to date has often de-emphasized arts education. But one result has been to illustrate how important it is for the arts to prove their value in the basic education of all children. It's true that the arts are now at the mercy of overburdened state and local education budgets. But in many states the result has been an intensification of efforts to link the arts to other state concerns.

The movement to include the arts in basic education is, in fact, gathering momentum in many states. If it can be demonstrated that arts education contributes to education reform overall, as many people are firmly convinced it can, then arts education can emerge from its current difficulties to play a stronger, more vital role in American education.

Figure 3
Legislative Appropriations to State Arts Agencies
Fiscal Year 1992

State or Territory	1992	State or Territory	1992
Alabama	$ 2,078,774	Nebraska	$ 1,184,703
Alaska	$ 1,194,500	Nevada	$ 518,745
American Samoa	$ 43,225	New Hampshire	$ 512,411
Arizona	$ 2,359,500	New Jersey	$ 10,271,000
Arkansas	$ 1,022,963	New Mexico	$ 1,307,400
California	$ 15,997,000	New York	$ 32,087,500
Colorado	$ 1,632,111	North Carolina	$ 4,683,566
Connecticut	$ 2,897,287	North Dakota	$ 289,533
Delaware	$ 1,331,900	Northern Marianas	$ 112,200
District of Columbia	$ 3,500,000	Ohio	$ 10,899,647
Florida	$ 16,527,388	Oklahoma	$ 3,457,572
Georgia	$ 3,059,070	Oregon	$ 1,399,189
Guam	$ 664,370	Pennsylvania	$ 9,773,000
Hawaii	$ 10,699,168	Puerto Rico	$ 10,697,714
Idaho	$ 744,600	Rhode Island	$ 942,536
Illinois	$ 8,829,900	South Carolina	$ 3,633,006
Indiana	$ 2,749,705	South Dakota	$ 407,527
Iowa	$ 1,170,027	Tennessee	$ 1,455,200
Kansas	$ 1,060,728	Texas	$ 3,260,516
Kentucky	$ 3,378,100	Utah	$ 2,016,900
Louisiana	$ 929,322	Vermont	$ 415,749
Maine	$ 660,040	Virgin Islands	$ 170,000
Maryland	$ 6,410,097	Virginia	$ 1,500,000
Massachusetts	$ 3,587,543	Washington	$ 2,372,240
Michigan	$ 4,200,000	West Virginia	$ 1,809,210
Minnesota	$ 4,018,000	Wisconsin	$ 2,956,300
Mississippi	$ 514,527	Wyoming	$ 340,699
Missouri	$ 4,012,684		
Montana	$ 959,433	TOTAL	$214,706,025

Source: National Assembly of State Arts Agencies

CHAPTER THREE

GETTING THERE

As education reform has swept through the states, the standards for arts education have become more rigorous, and there is a new emphasis on integrating the arts into education. Big challenges remain, though, in such areas as preparing teachers, improving the arts curriculum and its relationship to the curriculum overall, and assessing students' progress in the arts. Arts specialists in state departments of education, their counterparts in the state arts agencies, and many other people have been working hard to help school districts offer arts education. But often they simply have not been able to meet the mandates. Realizing the many benefits that art education brings will not occur until

• arts teachers (both art specialists and general classroom teachers) receive more and different training, that adequately equips them to use the arts in a comprehensive way;

• school districts develop standards to define an effective arts education curriculum, thereby providing teachers with sufficient direction about what they should teach;

• ways of incorporating the arts into the core curriculum for all students are created;

• schools decide what students should know and be able to do before graduating from high school and develop methods to adequately assess their progress.

This section presents a discussion of how states and school systems currently approach these troublesome practical issues. It also suggests ways to improve current arrangements so that the arts education delivered to students is more effective and better assessed.

Preparing Teachers

What makes a good teacher? Unfortunately, this simple question has no simple answer. According to the National Board for Professional Teaching Standards, the fundamental requirements for proficient teaching are relatively clear:

• Broad grounding in the liberal arts and sciences;

• Knowledge of the subjects to be taught, the skills to be developed, and the curricular arrangements and materials that organize and embody that content;

• Knowledge of general and subject-specific methods for teaching and for evaluating student learning;

• A knowledge of students and human development;

• Skills in effectively teaching students from racially, ethnically, and socioeconomically diverse backgrounds; and

• The skills, capacities, and dispositions to use such knowledge wisely in the interests of students.[1]

"The quality and success of arts education in the United States ultimately rests with those who teach the arts. It is the teachers who are responsible for fostering students' creativity and for conveying to them a sense of civilization."
—National Endowment for the Arts, *Toward Civilization*

As we shall see, however, the ways in which arts teachers are actually trained, certified, put to work in schools, and kept abreast of new developments in their fields are very different from state to state. In some ways, teachers are well prepared to teach the arts. In other ways, many people find room for considerable improvement.

Teacher Education

Teacher education has long been a predominant function of college and university arts schools. According to some experts, the U.S. system of preparing arts teachers stands out as a model. Robert Glidden, dean of the School of Music, Florida State University at Tallahassee, says, "We combine the study of one of the arts disciplines with liberal studies and professional education in a credit-packed baccalaureate education that overflows the traditional four-year boundaries. It is probably safe to say that nowhere else in the world has the preparation of arts teachers been taken so seriously or treated so systematically. From that perspective we must be considered very successful."

From another perspective, however, we could question whether any one of the components of the preparation of arts teachers—study of the art itself, liberal studies, professional education—is sufficient for today's schools.[2]

That question haunts teacher education generally. For a number of years, colleges and universities have been attacked as a weak link in the quest to improve schools. "Ninety percent of reality is in the perception," says Senator Wilhelmina Delco, Texas. "And the perception of teacher education is bad."

Even teachers criticize the training they receive. In 1991, Lou Harris polled 1,007 teachers who had just completed their first year of teaching, comparing their responses to what they had said before they began. Before: 81 percent said they were adequately prepared to teach, while only 70 percent still thought so after a year in the classroom.[3]

Part of the problem with teaching is that schools of education still do not attract the best and brightest high school and college students. That fact was highlighted in *A Nation at Risk*, which noted that many teachers were recruited from the bottom quarter of their classes. The states have taken a series of actions to correct this situation:

· Forty-five states limit entry to teacher-education programs or have strengthened

Tennessee: A Training Ground for Teachers

In Tennessee, teacher education receives the highest priority. The Comprehensive Education Reform Act of 1984, or CERA, was Tennessee's answer to education reform. Before CERA, funding for arts education was practically nonexistent, and most school systems did not employ elementary art and music specialists. Through CERA, Tennessee has increased funding for the arts and improved the delivery of comprehensive arts education.

In 1987, the state department of education created the Tennessee Arts Academy. The academy offers two one-week sessions, one on grades K-4, the second on grades 5 through 8, with separate tracks for arts specialists and general classroom teachers. Professional artists sponsored by the Tennessee Arts Commission participate with teachers in workshops on drama, the visual arts, and music.

Additionally, Tennessee hosts the Southeast Center for Education in the Arts. Housed at the University of Tennessee (Chattanooga), the Center is working toward comprehensive curriculum reform in and through the arts. Jeffrey Patchen, director of the center says, "Our goal is to improve the quality and quantity of arts education in the schools. We are working with all facets of the eduction system to effect long-term, meaningful change." To this end, the center works not only with teachers from the Southeast states (Tennessee, Georgia, Kentucky, Louisiana, and Virginia) but also with administrators, institutes of higher education, and arts specialists. Each summer, the center serves an average of 240 arts specialists, classroom teachers, and school principals. Patchen holds the only endowed chair in the arts in the country, a position funded in part with a $500 thousand allocation from the state legislature.

certification requirements.

· Twenty-one states require students to demonstrate a minimum level of competency on state tests before they enter a teacher education program.

· Fifteen states require students to have a minimum grade point average before they can matriculate in an education school.

· Twelve states require both a test and a minimum GPA.

The good news is that enrollment in college arts schools is on the rise. According to Bob Garwell, dean of the School of Fine Arts, Texas Christian University, "Teacher candidates see arts education as a major growth area in the public schools. There is a real demand for art teachers out there." He finds that the fine arts are even luring students away from the business schools. "There is a definite and well-documented trend here," says Garwell. "At TCU, the fine arts school has been surpassing the business school in enrollment for the last three years."

Certification

Most art and music teachers today have graduated from professional teacher preparation programs or have passed a state test. Every state in the nation offers a certificate for visual art; 24 states certify theater teachers, and 16 certify dance teachers.[4] (Theater teachers are often certified through the English department and dance teachers are certified through the physical education department.) In 49 states, teachers receive certificates that let them teach art in all grades; in 21 states teachers can be certified specifically for elementary school, for elementary and junior high school, or for high school.

Some school districts, particularly in affluent communities, hire art and music teachers for elementary schools. Generally, though, elementary schools are much less likely than secondary schools to employ specialists. This means that teaching the arts often becomes the responsibility of elementary school teachers who are expected to teach all the other subjects as well. Yet, as we shall see, their training in the arts varies widely from state to state.

Most states require teachers to complete a specific number of credit hours in the arts for certification, and most elementary school teachers have had a least one course in music or visual art as part of their undergraduate education. Some states require that teachers take only a general course in teaching the arts, though others require further training in art or music.

One problem is that the courses sometimes amount to little more than simple "art making" or singing and rarely reflect a comprehensive approach to teaching art or demonstrate how the arts integrate with other subjects. Another difficulty is that teachers who have very little education in the arts are not comfortable teaching them, especially when the arts are to be integrated into the basic curriculum. They are like teachers trained in physical education, who often feel unprepared

State Museum Reaches Out to Teachers

In Florida, the Legislature appropriates $1.6 million per year to support the John and Mable Ringling Museum of Art. Since 1987 the Ringling has conducted teacher outreach programs to help faculty learn how to use the museum as a teaching resource. Workshops in discipline-based art education conducted in partnership with the Florida Institute for Art Education provide an opportunity for teachers to learn as well as ways to teach art as a separate discipline like history or science.

to teach dance and movement when what they know most about is football and basketball.

Teachers who are certified as arts specialists are in a somewhat different situation. They are usually certified in a single arts discipline, and they must meet standards (set by the National Association of Schools of Arts and Design, the National Association of Schools of Dance, the National Association of Schools of Music, or the National Association of Schools of Theater) that generally recommend they take at least half their college course work in the discipline they plan to teach.

The problem in this case is not the education of arts specialists but the fact that relatively few schools are able to employ them. Most experts in arts education agree that art is best taught by certified specialists. But nearly half (42 percent) of the nation's elementary schools have no visual arts specialist, and 32 percent have a specialist only part time. Only 26 percent have a full-time specialist. The picture is brighter for music specialists. Nearly half of all elementary schools (45 percent) are served by full-time music specialists, and 39 percent are served part time; only 16 percent do not have music specialists.

Changes in Certification

The examinations that arts teachers now take to become certified generally use multiple-choice questions to test technical information, knowledge of the history of the art form, and familiarity with teaching procedures. The National Endowment for the Arts recommends the use of comprehensive examinations instead. These examinations would test competence in teaching the arts, in planning comprehensive units of instruction, and in teaching art history, and art criticism as well as the production or performance of art.

Some states are already introducing new examinations. Florida, for example, has new tests that have been developed using the expertise of K-12 teachers and that prepare teachers for what is "relevant and important" by testing more than minimum qualifications.[5] The fine arts test is one of 48 tests that were developed in response to the Legislature's 1986 mandate that practicing teachers and instructors new to the state pass an examination certifying their competence to teach in their subject area. So far, though, there is no real agreement on how effective the test is in selecting Florida's future teachers. In fact, most teachers and administrators report that the test has raised more questions than it has answered.

As states revise their procedures for certifying teachers, there is also a movement to set national standards for teachers. Among the many advocates of this idea is the Carnegie Commission, which has created the National Board for Professional Teaching Standards. The board is creating arts standards that all teachers and school boards respect and ways to measure how well teachers meet them. The goal is for "board-certified" to become "an unambiguous statement that its holder is a highly qualified teacher."[6]

Table 1
State Teacher Certification Requirements for Art Teachers

State	Elementary						Secondary					
	Arts in General	Creative Writing	Dance	Drama	Music	Visual Art	Arts in General	Creative Writing	Dance	Drama	Music	Visual Art
Alabama	x				x	x					x	x
Alaska												
American Samoa												
Arizona					x	x	x	x	x	x	x	x
Arkansas					x	x					x	x
California							x	x	x	x	x	x
Colorado	x				x		x			x	x	
Connecticut					x	x					x	x
Delaware		x			x	x		x		x	x	x
District of Columbia					x	x					x	x
Florida	x	x	x	x	x	x	x	x	x	x	x	x
Georgia			x	x	x	x			x	x	x	x
Hawaii											x	x
Idaho					x	x				x	x	x
Illinois	x				x	x	x				x	x
Indiana	x				x	x	x				x	x
Iowa					x	x				x	x	x
Kansas			x		x	x				x	x	x
Kentucky					x	x					x	x
Louisiana					x	x					x	x
Maine	x				x		x				x	
Maryland			x	x	x	x			x	x	x	x
Massachusetts			x	x	x	x			x	x	x	x
Michigan	x		x		x	x	x		x		x	x
Minnesota					x	x					x	x
Mississippi			x		x	x					x	x
Missouri					x	x					x	x
Montana					x	x					x	x
Nebraska	x			x	x	x	x			x	x	x
Nevada	x				x	x	x			x	x	x
New Hampshire					x	x					x	x
New Jersey	x			x	x	x	x			x	x	
New Mexico					x	x				x	x	x
New York					x	x					x	x
North Carolina			x	x	x	x				x	x	x
North Dakota	x				x	x	x				x	x
Ohio			x		x	x				x	x	x
Oklahoma			x		x	x				x	x	x
Oregon					x	x					x	x
Pennsylvania	x	x	x	x	x	x	x	x	x	x	x	x
Puerto Rico			x		x	x				x	x	x
Rhode Island			x		x	x			x		x	x
South Carolina	x				x		x				x	
South Dakota	x				x		x				x	
Tennessee					x	x					x	x
Texas			x		x	x			x	x	x	x
Utah					x				x	x	x	x
Vermont					x	x			x		x	x
Virginia					x	x				x	x	x
Virgin Islands	x				x	x	x				x	x
Washington					x		x				x	
West Virginia					x	x				x	x	x
Wisconsin			x	x	x	x	x			x	x	
Wyoming	x				x							
TOTAL	16	3	11	13	50	42	18	5	16	24	52	45

Note: Many states provide K-12 certification per subject area, without distinguishing between elementary and secondary levels. For those states, a symbol appears in both elementary and secondary columns above.
Source: Council of Chief State School Officers

Table 2

Elementary schools in districts served by visual arts and music specialists: 1986–1987

| District characteristic | Percentage of schools served | | | | | |
| | Visual arts specialists | | | Music specialist | | |
	Served full-time	Served part-time	Not Served	Served full-time	Served part-time	Not Served
All districts	26	32	42	45	39	16
Enrollment size						
Less than 2,500	22	29	49	43	36	21
2,500 to 9,999	29	37	34	42	44	15
10,000 or more	28	30	42	51	37	12
Metropolitan status						
Urban	32	35	33	39	48	13
Suburban	32	28	40	57	32	11
Rural	19	34	47	37	41	22
Geographic Region						
Northeast	50	35	15	60	37	3
Central	26	30	44	46	35	19
Southeast	16	39	44	39	41	20
West	16	26	58	37	42	21

Source: Music Educators National Conference

Ongoing Teacher Education

Though in-service training is commonplace in many school systems, some people charge that continuing education occurs with less frequency in the arts than in other subject areas.[7] Where in-service training in the arts is available, it is often planned and implemented with the help of the state department of education and professional arts organizations like the Alliance for Arts in Education.

In New Jersey, for example, the state's Alliance for Arts Education and the state arts agency each year sponsor a week-long conference for arts teachers and administrators. The participants receive "cross-discipline" training. In other words, visual arts teachers learn about dance and music teaching methods. Elsewhere, institutions of higher education help organize yearly conferences on the arts (see SIDEBAR).

Less common than continued training for teachers, but also valuable, is training in the arts for principals and other administrators. If principals are convinced of the importance of the arts, they can share this conviction with teachers. Their support for the arts will be especially vital where site-based management gives them more power over the curriculum.

The Special Case of Artists in Residence

Schools also draw on the services of professional artists who have an interest in working in education settings. These artists in residence, who often bring the arts to schools where cultural experiences are not readily available, are an important resource for teachers. Administration of the "Artists-In-Schools" (AIS) program is the responsibility of state arts agencies.

According to the National Association of State Arts Agencies, all states have a residency program, and these programs have proved enormously popular. In Montana, for example, where the program began in 1970 with 11 poets visiting fewer than 20 schools, more than 150 elementary schools, high schools, colleges, and arts centers now host residencies in the visual arts, creative writing, theater, dance, film and video, music, and folk arts. In Massachusetts, the legislature funds the residency program, supplying money that the arts agency uses to support a full staff of education professionals.

AIS programs operate under guidelines that generally include a statement like the following from the Pennsylvania Council on the Arts: "Artists should not be considered members of the teaching staff while in residence at a school, and are not to be assigned as substitute teachers. Teachers MUST be in the classroom at all times participating in the activities."[8] Even where the guidelines are followed, though, some people see drawbacks to the AIS programs. The major objection is that visiting artists cannot provide the consistent contact students need.

**Live from New York,
the Lincoln Center Institute**

The Lincoln Center Institute has served as a model for many state training programs. A three-week summer session conducted by teaching artists in dance, music, theater, and film, the Institute is held at the Juilliard School in cooperation with the Teachers College of Columbia University. Participants (three elementary teachers and five high school teachers from each school district) see live performances, receive intensive teacher training, and design programs for their students.

Changing The Curriculum

Education reform has supplied a push for rigorous standards in arts education. States have responded by changing graduation requirements and working with school districts to change the arts curriculum. Now, though, it is becoming clear that substantially improving students' preparation in the arts will require more work in both areas.

Graduation Requirements

Almost all states—42 in all—require school districts to offer arts instruction in elementary, middle, or secondary school. Although fewer states require arts courses for graduation, that number has risen dramatically since 1980, when only two states included the arts in graduation requirements.

Unfortunately, establishing graduation requirements in the arts has not necessarily given all students an opportunity to receive a good education in the arts. One problem has been that the requirements are sometimes loosely defined. In 13 states, for example, courses in domestic science, industrial arts, humanities, foreign languages, or computer sciences are acceptable alternatives to arts classes.

Further, many college-bound students have little incentive to take arts courses since few colleges accept them for credit. This situation may be changing, however. In some states now, study in the arts is a requirement for college entrance and college graduation. In Tennessee, for example, students will soon be required to take one unit of "fine arts" in high school to enter any Tennessee public university, and even the community colleges will recommend that applicants take fine arts. The requirement takes effect in fall of 1993. Before it does, the Arts Task Force of the Tennessee Collaborative for Educational Excellence will review the K-12 arts curriculum to decide which fine arts courses will satisfy the new requirement and to ensure that those courses teach basic academic competencies.[9]

Responding to new state graduation requirements has challenged school districts. They must revise their courses to comply with the new regulations, but often they do not dedicate the resources necessary to hire arts specialists, develop curriculum, or buy materials. The requirements often frustrate arts specialists, too, who must cope with higher enrollment. Take the situation of the visual arts teacher in Ohio who found that teaching artistically gifted students in the lower grades had to give way to teaching seniors fulfilling a requirement. Comments the teacher, "To make this requirement work, schools are going to have to hire more classroom teachers."

Curriculum Guides

A further problem made more apparent by higher graduation requirements is the lack of agreement about what required courses should cover. With the possible exception of music

Texas Trains Artists to Teach

After Texas in 1983 began requiring that the arts be part of basic education, it faced a shortage of arts teachers. So, in 1990, it established the Artists Training Institute. From a state roster of artists in education, the Texas Commission on the Arts identified artists to participate in the institute. There the artists learn how a typical classroom works, what restraints they face, and how to integrate arts lessons with general instruction.

Table 3
States with Graduation Requirements in the Arts
(in Carnegie course units)

State	Number	Subject
Arkansas*	.5	Drama, music, visual arts
California	1	Fine arts (creative writing, dance, drama, music, visual arts), or foreign language
	2	California requires 2 for college bound students
Connecticut	1	Arts (dance, drama, music, visual arts), or vocational education
Florida*	.5	Fine arts (dance, drama, music, visual arts), vocational education, or computer technology
Hawaii	1	For academic honors only (art or music)
Idaho	.5	Fine arts (creative writing, dance, drama, music, visual arts), foreign language, or humanities
Indiana	2	For students seeking an honors diploma
Louisiana	.5	For students in the Regents Program (typically, the college-bound)
Maine	1	Fine arts (visual arts, music, drama), or forensics
Maryland*	1	Fine arts (dance, drama, music, visual arts)
Missouri*	1	Music or visual arts
New Hampshire*	.5	Arts education (art, music, visual arts, dance, drama)
New Jersey	1	Fine arts, practical arts, or performing arts
New Mexico	.5	Fine arts (visual arts, music, dance, drama), practical arts, or vocational education
New York*	1	Dance, drama, music, or visual arts
Nevada	1	Fine arts or humanities
North Carolina	1	For students enrolled in the Scholars Program
Oregon	1	Music, visual arts, foreign language, or vocational education
Pennsylvania	2	Arts (dance, drama, music, visual arts), or humanities
Rhode Island	.5	For college-bound students only—dance, drama, music, or visual arts
South Dakota*	.5	Fine arts (dance, drama, music, visual arts)
	1	South Dakota requires 1 for college-bound students
Tennessee	2	For students seeking an honors diploma
Texas	1	For advanced academic program students only—drama, music, or visual arts
Utah*	1.5	Dance, drama, music, or visual arts
Vermont*	1	General arts, dance, drama, music, or visual arts
Virginia	1	Fine arts (art, music, dance, theater), or practical arts
West Virginia	1	Music, visual arts, or applied arts

*States that require some study of the arts by every high school student.
This table is a revision of one first published in *Arts, Education and the States: A Survey of State Education Policies* (Washington, D.C.: Council of Chief State School Officers, 1985), updated with information from the National Art Education Association; Alliance for Arts Education; The John F. Kennedy Center for the Performing Arts; and the National Assembly of State Arts Agencies.

education, there are comparatively few textbooks in the arts to guide teachers, and there is little continuity in the arts education curriculum. Though the experts agree that curriculum improvement is essential, they disagree about what should be taught. When former Secretary of Education William Bennett proposed a model high school curriculum in 1987, he suggested that high school students complete a minimum of one semester each in art history and music history. But the model curriculum made no mention of theater, dance, design, and media arts—an omission that other experts considered serious.

Developing a comprehensive, basic, sequential program for K-12 students is an enormous task. Many states have begun to address it by developing curriculum frameworks to guide schools. According to the Council of Chief State School Officers, 36 states provide curriculum guidelines and supplementary information in visual art, 34 in music, 20 in theater, and 18 in dance.[10]

According to a review by the National Endowment for the Arts, state curriculum guidelines are generally well balanced. They include
• broadening the student's understanding of the role that the arts play in cultural heritage;
• developing the student's ability to make judgments on the quality of works of visual art and music;
• developing the student's ability to perform and create art or music;
• generating an understanding of the basic elements of visual art or music.

Locally, most districts have curriculum guides that set goals for "student outcomes." Though 75 percent of school districts have music guides for all grade levels, only 35 percent have guides for dance, drama, and creative writing in the elementary grades.

Unfortunately, state and local guidelines are often not followed. Sometimes they are not comprehensive enough to provide real guidance; sometimes they do not draw on the most respected theoretical thinking.[11] Guidelines are generally written by arts specialists for other arts specialists, so they sometimes fail to provide general classroom teachers with appropriate direction.

Guidelines create further difficulties, according to former NEA chairman Frank Hodsell. "The single greatest drawback of existing arts curricula and teachers' guides is their emphasis on skill development at the expense of the

Outcomes of the Music Program

The Music Educators National Conference says that the fundamental purpose of teaching music in the schools is to develop in each student, as fully as possible, the ability to create, and understand music. Instruction in music should lead to specific skills and knowledge. The elementary and secondary music program should be designed to produce individuals who
• are able to make music, alone and with others;
• are able to improvise and create music;
• are able to use the vocabulary and notation of music;
• are able to respond to music aesthetically, intellectually, and emotionally;
• are acquainted with a wide variety of music, including diverse musical styles and genres;
• understand the role music has played and continues to play in the lives of human beings;
• are able to make aesthetic judgments based on critical listening and analysis;
• have developed a commitment to music;
• support the musical life of the community and encourage others to do so;
• are able to continue their musical learning independently.

These outcomes apply to the student who has received only the required instruction. Students who have taken elective courses in music will have developed certain specialized skills and knowledge to a higher degree.

TEACHING TALENTED STUDENTS

When gifted students can develop their talents they can take advantage of opportunities like performing with a renowned ballet company during their summer vacations. Although most schools can't offer more than basic physical education, some parents, school administrators, and state legislators have worked to develop special schools that train artistically talented children.

Most of these schools are small, serving no more than about 500 students. In addition to teaching students standard academic subjects, they usually offer a curriculum that includes visual art, dance, theater, and sometimes creative writing. Some are residential schools, full-time public or private boarding schools that recruit both in-state and out-of-state students and may also run a "day" program. Nonresidential schools for the arts, or "magnet" schools, are usually in metropolitan areas and are usually public. Nonresidential "arts only" schools offer half-day programs for students who spend the other half-day in their home schools. Some arts schools are actually "schools within schools," a smaller program within a larger school. Increasingly popular in recent years have been residential summer schools of the arts, such as governors' summer schools in the arts or summer programs on college campuses. Many summer programs have now expanded into year-long programs.

The oldest special school for the arts is the High School of Music and Art in New York City, which was founded in 1938. But with the recent growth of legislative interest in magnet schools generally and arts schools specifically, at least 37 states now have these special schools, according to the National Art Education Association.

• The North Carolina School of the Arts, now nationally known, began in 1965 with an appropriation from the state legislature. Today the school serves more than 700 students from 46 states and 11 countries. They study music, dance, drama, design and production, and visual arts.

• In 1986 the Illinois Legislature passed the Summer School for the Arts Act. The purpose of the school is to "serve the people of Illinois as a place to nourish the creativity of its youth who possess outstanding talent in the various arts areas, and to return these young people to their home community better prepared to make a contribution to the cultural opportunities available in their town."(HB 3550, 1986) In addition to providing excellence in arts education, the school is to serve as a model for the development of innovative instructional techniques and curricula.

As exciting as these special schools are, they tend to reinforce the belief that arts are only for the gifted and talented. Some people charge that these schools siphon off gifted students and teachers who could enrich other schools and many fear that policymakers who fund magnet schools will conclude that the arts in education have been adequately addressed.

The notion that special schools are not a substitute for including the arts in the general education of every child has led to controversies in states. In Minnesota, for example, in 1985 the Legislature appropriated $500,000 to start the Minnesota School of the Arts. The school received an additional $2 million in 1987 and the opportunity to take over a defunct college campus. It opened its doors in 1989 with a junior class of 135 and an annual budget of $6 million. Though the school has been successful, many arts educators and policymakers questioned its high-profile mission and budget, arguing that the $6 million would have been better spent bringing the arts to every student. The Alliance for Arts Education endorsed the school only after it was agreed that it would serve as a resource for the entire state, not just Minneapolis/St. Paul. The school further agreed to share its experience in using the arts as a tool to teach other academic subjects.

Figure 4
South Carolina Curriculum Goals

Creative writing should, but not be restricted to, fiction, poetry, non-fiction, and playwriting. A curriculum in creative writing should attain the following educational goals:

Channel the creative possibilities in various genres—"creative expression."

Discover the cultural history of discipline through studies, including classic, modern, and contemporary writers—"cultural heritage."

Develop the ability to analyze and critique in each genre—"aesthetic valuing."

Dance education should include, but not be restricted to, creative movement, ballet, modern, jazz, folk dance, choreography, and improvisation. A curriculum in dance should attain the following goals:

Develop body movement beginning with creative movement at the lower grades and progress to formal technique study in the upper grades. The elements and sub-elements of movements: THE BODY (parts and body moves, including locomotor and axial), SPACE (shape, level, direction, size, focus, place, and pathway), FORCE (heavy, light, bound-free), and TIME (beat accent, speed, duration, and rhythmic pattern).

Develop the ability to recognize significant dance works and factors which make them significant. Develop an understanding of the socio-historical context in which dance emerged.

Develop perceptual and critical skills through the observation of significant works.

Music education should include, but not be restricted to, singing, playing musical instruments, band, and chorus. A curriculum in music should attain the following educational goals:

Develop expressive skills that include singing, playing, conducting, and writing music.

Develop sound production, the elements of music, and the structure and form of music.

Develop an understanding of musical heritage, the expressive elements of the music of other cultures, and the social and historical influences on music composition, style, and performance.

Visual Arts education should include, but not be restricted to, drawing, painting, printmaking, sculpture, photography, pottery. A curriculum in art should attain the following educational goals:

Develop skills to express and communicate responses to experiences.

Develop an understanding of the environment in terms of visual and tactile experiences.

Develop an understanding of historical and cultural developments that occur as a result of varying needs and aesthetic points of view.

Develop a base for making informed aesthetic judgments.

Drama/theater education should include, but not be restricted to, acting, directing, mime, improvisation, design and technical production (scenery, costume, lighting, make-up, sound), theater history, and dramatic literature. A drama/theater curriculum should attain the following goals:

Develop observational and perceptual skills for recognizing and comprehending the concepts and structures that underlie dramatic art.

Develop muscular coordination and physical and emotional control in structured and in improvisational situations as preparation for individual and cooperative group exploration and expression within a dramatic framework.

Develop skills to read, analyze, and interpret literary art throughout history and across cultures and thereby to understand ourselves and our heritage.

Develop knowledge and skills for critical evaluation and thus enhance the appreciation and enjoyment of all dramatic forms.

Source: ABC Plan, South Carolina Department of Education, 1991.

art form as a whole," he says. "The problem is that the specific learning objectives do not reflect the balance contained in the (NEA) goals. Rather, they tend to emphasize the last goal, learning the elements of the art's forms, over study of works of art. The result is that the goals tend to be obscured in a sea of narrowly focused 'skill' outcomes."[12]

An approach to curriculum that is receiving national attention is the comprehensive approach to arts education (sometimes referred to as DBAE). As we saw in Part I, this curriculum adds the study of art history, art criticism, and aesthetics to the production of art. The curriculum is written, sequential, and carried out in entire schools or districts. In contrast to the traditional approach of limiting art to art making, discipline-based arts education programs are reinforced (or sustained by) sequential curriculum that is delivered in a variety of ways. Central to this approach is that the arts are basic to the curriculum for all students. The best of these programs are coordinated by district arts specialists who work with individual classroom teachers.

Some states have begun to give the arts curriculum serious attention.

• In California, the *Visual Arts Framework for the California Public Schools, Kindergarten Through Grade Twelve*, published in 1982 and updated in 1989 to include all the arts, helps curriculum planners design a curriculum for dance, drama, music, and visual arts. It also gives guidelines for textbook publishers, for whom California, with its large population and centralized selection of textbooks, is a major market. The goals of the California framework are to develop the unique characteristics of each of the arts, integrate the arts, and correlate the arts with the general curriculum.

• In Illinois, the state department of education worked with the Illinois Alliance for Arts Education to develop learning objectives for students.

• Florida's State Board of Education has adopted curriculum frameworks that reflect the DBAE approach. With money from the Getty Center for Education in the Arts, the Division of Cultural Affairs, the Jessie Ball du Pont Fund, and the Division of Public Schools, teachers and administrators from 18 school systems have been trained in DBAE at the Florida Institute for Art Education at Florida State University.

Assessing Student Learning

In the last 10 years, state policymakers have been awash in a sea of statistics comparing American students to students in the rest of the world. Legislators cope with questions of how their state compares with neighboring

World Class Standards in the Arts

The National Standards for Education in the Arts project, sponsored by the U.S. Department of Education, the National Endowment for the Humanities, and the National Endowment for the Arts, is in the process of developing standards for each of the four arts disciplines: music, art, theater, and dance in grades preK - 12. Development of world-class standards in the arts is the centerpiece of the seven-component America 2000 Arts Partnership.

The push for national standards began in January 1992, when the National Council on Education Standards and Testing (NCEST) called for a system of voluntary national standards and assessments in the "core" subjects of math, English, science, history, and geography, with "other subjects to follow." The arts are the first of the "other subjects" to receive federal funding.

The Consortium of Arts Education Associations, American Alliance for Theater and Education, Music Educators National Conference, National Art Education Association, and the National Dance Association, will develop standards for each discipline that also consider the special needs of children from diverse cultural backgrounds and children with disabilities. The final recommendations will be released in the summer of 1993.—Consortium of National Arts Education Associations

states, or how "good" certain school districts are. Parents everywhere, like parents in Garrison Keillor's Lake Wobegon, want every child to be above average. Across the board, legislators, parents, and other constituents are demanding accountability in education.

Less clear than the widespread desire for measurable results in education is exactly what "accountability" means and how it is to be achieved. The situation in arts education is especially complicated, since it is more difficult to measure achievement in the arts in a subject like mathematics, and it is, in fact, measured much less frequently.

Trends in Accountability

Fueling the interest in new forms of assessment have been rising expectations about what assessment can accomplish.[13] In earlier times, the primary purpose of assessment was to gather data on how well schools were doing. Now, though, states are tying the results of assessment to student promotion and graduation. Traditional subject areas, even mathematics, are being expanded to include topics such as conceptualization, problem-solving, and complex cognitive skills—skills that are difficult to evaluate with a multiple-choice test.

Multiple-choice tests have been criticized for other failings as well. They measure the wrong skills and are simplistic, say the critics. They put a premium on memorization and test-taking skills. When a "school report card" or some other sort of public report is based on the results of a standardized test, teachers tend to teach to the test. The tests may be biased in favor of white, middle-class students. They easily lend themselves to cheating. In sum, say the critics, standardized multiple-choice tests are not "authentic" measures of achievement.

Nor have the results of these tests been used properly, goes the argument. According to a widely cited study by testing critic John J. Cannell, all 50 states reported that their students scored above the national average on standardized commercial achievement tests.[14]

For all these reasons, interest is growing in new measures of student performance. Perhaps the most popular new form of assessment that is emerging from the education reform movement is "outcomes-based" assessment or "performance assessment." Performance tests intend to

States Assess Performance

Michigan, through its Michigan Educational Assessment Program (MEAP), has been a leader in performance assessment for more than years. Performance assessments are administered to students in ma matics, music, science, social studies, art, music, career developmen and physical education.

A pioneer in the incorporation of performance-based assessmen into the core curriculum, Vermont will be the first state to use portfo in addition to standardized tests. The state plans to assess students the fourth and eighth grades in writing and mathematics in three wa uniform tests, a portfolio that includes material collected during the year, and a "best piece" that represents what a student considers his her best effort.

The "Essential Learner Outcomes Assessments" commit Minneso using some form of performance-based assessment at each grade lev and in each subject. Minnesota is also the first state to legislate out comes-based "charter schools." Certified teachers will create and op ate eight of these schools, which will be public—free and available to eligible students—but exempt from most state regulations. All aspec the education program will be determined by the schools' board of directors, most of whom must be teachers. The only restriction on c riculum is that it must be outcomes-based. California and Colorado a also exploring the charter school idea.

California has led the nation in the development of "authentic" te ing. It now uses a combination of open-ended questions, portfolios, "investigations" to test students in mathematics, for example, and pl to use a similar combination in science, history, and the other social ences. Investigations, which last 40 to 60 minutes, are problem-solv projects conducted by students either individually or in small groups The investigations are administered by trained classroom teachers.

assess how well students apply their learning to real-life tasks.[15] They require students to demonstrate competence rather than simply to select one of several predetermined answers to an exercise.

A popular form of performance assessment is the portfolio. Following a procedure that has always been used in the arts, students are evaluated on the basis of work which they themselves select. Portfolios are now being used to assess students in writing, mathematics, the arts, and other subjects.

The new techniques offer advantages, especially because they can measure outcomes that are difficult to assess any other way, like analytic and problem-solving skills. They do, however, take more time than multiple-choice tests, and they cost more. Computer scoring machines cannot be used, so grading may be subjective and, therefore, inconsistent.

In sum, states are finding that performance tests, portfolios, investigations, and other new forms of assessment are not problem-free, but they are promising.

Accountability in Arts Education

Current thinking suggests that the best assessment not only indicates what the students know and understand about art, but also points out to teachers the strengths and weaknesses of the curriculum and of the instruction.

Unfortunately, many schools have little or no idea what their students are learning in the arts. According to the NEA, only about 6 percent of school districts require competency tests in the arts for promotion to the next grade. Many states and districts are seeking to change this by mandating competency tests.

Some problems of testing are unique to the arts. First, there is a lack of standardized curricula, texts, and resource materials. Second, the arts (especially the visual arts) do not readily lend themselves to easily scored testing formats. Perhaps most important, there is disagreement in the professional arts community over whether testing is a good idea.

Opposing testing in the arts are people who feel that the arts are too different from other school subjects to be measured by the same academic standards. Some teachers say that "the arts are too subtle, too value-laden, too individual, too pervaded with aesthetic qualities, too open-ended, too unpredictable to be tested or assessed." Other critics of testing fear that dissecting the works art students create and perform "can actually destroy the things we love and hope to encourage."[16]

In favor of testing in the arts are people like the school administrators and arts professionals who participated in a 1991 symposium on arts education assessment sponsored by the Council of Chief State School Officers and the National Endowment for the Arts. They cited the following reasons for testing the arts:
• What gets tested gets taught. Subjects that schools do not test are seen as unimportant and

"Testing and assessment in education can be either a blessing or a curse. Good educational assessment is useful, and bad assessment is useless, worthless, and deceptive. With good comprehensive assessment programs, arts education could be improved markedly; with bad assessment, arts education could be damaged and made trivial."
—Brent Wilson, Pennsylvania State University

expendable in tough times. If the arts are to become essential components of general education, they must be tested like any other subject.

• Testing produces measurable goals. School administrators need test results to gauge the effectiveness of the curriculum in meeting the goals of comprehensive arts education. So do parents, administrators, supervisors, and public officials.

• Effective tests give teachers information they need to strengthen the curriculum and otherwise improve student learning and their own teaching.

• Good assessment techniques are available now. Techniques already being used to assess music and the visual arts are actually so effective that they have served as models for other subjects. These techniques need only be formalized and put into coherent assessment programs.[17]

One indication of growing interest in testing student achievement in the arts is the decision by the National Assessment of Educational Progress (NAEP) to include performance-based assessment of the visual arts and music education in its 1994 tests. This is a revival of sorts for NAEP, which tested students in both fields in the 1970s.

Interest in performance-based assessment of students' knowledge of the arts is strong in the states as well.

• In Minnesota, the department of education is following the NAEP model by undertaking a systematic, continuous, census-like survey of knowledge, skills, understanding, and attitudes at three age levels across 10 subject areas. This plan reduces the costs of developing and scoring assessment exercises and allows Minnesota to compare results with results elsewhere. Beginning in 1989, the state Legislature required school districts to use the assessment instruments to measure students' progress toward "essential learner outcome" (ELO) goals. The tests are administered to a statewide sample of 18,000 to 20,000 students every year.

The ELO tests will be piloted in the visual arts in 1992 for grades 5, 8, and 11. The assessments will measure perceiving and understanding of art; knowledge of its cultural and historical contexts; problem-finding in art; development and transformation of ideas through art; art production and skills development; and spatial representation, visual sensitivity, and communication through arts. ELO tests in music will be piloted in 1993.[18]

• In 1977, the Maryland State Board of Education mandated K-8 experiences in art, music, dance, and drama, adding a fine arts credit requirement and electives

What Makes an Effective Test?

The National Forum on Assessment suggests that effective tests meet eight criteria.

1. Educational standards specifying what students should know and be able to do should be clearly defined before assessment procedures and exercises are developed.

2. The primary purpose of the assessment systems should be to assist both educators and policymakers to improve instruction and advance student learning.

3. Assessment standards, tasks, procedures, and uses should be fair to all students.

4. The assessment or tasks should be valid and appropriate representations of the standards students are expected to achieve.

5. Assessment results should be reported in the context of other relevant information.

6. Teachers should be involved in designing and using the assessment system.

7. Assessment procedures and results should be understandable.

8. The assessment system should be subject to continuous review and improvement—The National Forum on Assessment, *Criteria for Evaluation of Student Assessment Systems*

Figure 5
Selected Portfolio Artwork

Hwa Jung, Gardena High School
Teacher: Nancy McDonald

Hwa Jung Answers a Student Survey on Portfolio Assessment

"The portfolio is a good way of thinking and seeing what I learned in art, because I can compare my artwork each time. In the portfolio, I was pleased with the grade since I tended to work harder and thus get a good grade as a result. I learned that the portfolio can help me get a lot of experience that helps me. Every time I can see that I'm getting better work than old work, and also I can find what was wrong with my work. I want to keep a portfolio again because it helps me grow in my art skills. My teacher was able to make me do a variety of artwork and we could discuss about my works much easier just by reviewing my portfolio. With the portfolio I could develop my own style and way of keeping the portfolio and make significant progress. I kept track where I was and it was very helpful."

Hwa has been in the United States for only 1½ years. She was in the English as a Second Language program until this past spring semester when she was enrolled in all regular classes for the first time.

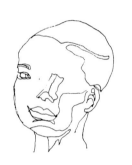 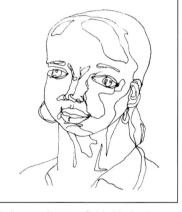  

1. *This was the first step of the contour drawing.*
I had some new experiences with this drawing.
I learned how to use the line control of shape on the subject. Also it helped my artwork skills.

2. *I was so happy to finish this drawing because it was so difficult to express the different volume of the face.*

3. *When I practiced drawing, I felt like I was getting better at drawing. This is the practice of the seated figure of my classmate. This time I tried to get a close picture and also to use delicate line to express more like a real person.*

4. *This is the final drawing of the seated figure. I must say it is very interesting. I like the expression of the shape and proportion of the figure in this drawing.*

Source: California Art Education Association, *A Visual Arts Portfolio Assessment Pilot Project.*

in 1987. Because arts education in Maryland is discipline-based, students are expected to meet goals in aesthetic experience, creative expression, cultural heritage, and criticism. They are to meet these goals when they leave grades three, five, eight, and 11.[19]

• In 1985, the California Legislature passed Senate Bill 813, which requires high school graduates to complete one year of visual or performing arts or foreign languages. In 1987, the California State University system revised its entrance requirements to include one year of visual or performing arts. The Legislature's statewide plan, *Strengthening the Arts in California Schools: A Design for the Future*, recommends that the state testing program expand to cover the visual and performing arts. Last year, Senator Gary Hart sponsored Senate Bill 662, which seeks to determine how well students in grades 4, 5, 8, and 10 meet statewide performance standards. Education officials are now developing tests for the arts and vocational education.[20]

• The New York State Education Department is working with the New York Art Teachers Association to assess performance in the arts. A primary goal is finding ways to help teachers review portfolios while permitting students of different disciplines, cultural backgrounds, and abilities to demonstrate their knowledge.

Even as states improve assessment procedures, discussions continue about the feasibility and propriety of developing a national framework for assessment that would cover arts education. Many legislators, teachers, and administrators have voiced concern that national goals are inappropriate and take away the discretion of states and school districts. But many educators and administrators favor the idea. For example, both the National Endowment for the Arts and the Council of Chief State School Officers favor national goals if the process for developing them is open and inclusive. The theory is that setting national goals for arts education could help state policymakers make a good case for programs that otherwise might be lost.

four

To demonstrate how policymakers can support arts education, finance arts initiatives, and use the arts to enhance other academic disciplines, this chapter presents case studies of arts education in four states—Minnesota, New Jersey, Oklahoma, and South Carolina.

Each case-study state has made a statewide commitment to arts education. Some other similarities are a dedication to providing arts education to all students, a belief that the arts should be a part of the basic curriculum, and a discipline-based approach to teaching the arts. Also, each state has had to wrestle with the issue of how to assess student learning in the arts.

Still, the real reason for highlighting these states is that each has a unique approach to arts education. To provide "all the arts for all the kids," Minnesota has set up a Comprehensive Arts Planning Program, and its commitment to outcome-based education has been a plus for the arts. New Jersey legislators created the Literacy in the Arts Task Force to assess arts education in the state and recommend improvements. Policymakers in Oklahoma have made the arts as basic to education as math and science in their comprehensive education reform legislation. South Carolina's Target 2000 School Reform Act includes art education legislation and the Arts in Basic Curriculum Plan, and the state has been a leader in, for example, developing curriculum frameworks for the arts.

Minnesota: All the Arts for All the Kids

Minnesota's most sweeping program, the Comprehensive Arts Planning Program (CAPP), provides widespread benefits for a limited investment. Supported through legislation and state appropriations, CAPP is the mainstay of Minnesota's arts education plan. In 1985, the Minnesota Legislature established the Minnesota Center for Arts Education, to oversee the state's residential arts high school and to provide financial and other resources for arts education throughout the state. The arts high school embraces outcome-based education, a system that works particularly well in the arts and strengthens their intellectual legitimacy.

The Comprehensive Arts Planning Program (CAPP)

Minnesota's Comprehensive Arts Planning Program, which was initiated in 1983, helps selected school districts create and carry out comprehensive arts programs. Each CAPP district receives special funding for two years. During the first year, the district develops a five-year, long-range plan; funding for year two is not allocated until this plan is complete. In the second year, the district receives technical assistance in such matters

> "The arts teach skills that are necessary to the development of "whole persons"—thoughtful, open, creative citizens and leaders"—*Comprehensive Arts Planning Manual, Minnesota.*

as tackling financial issues, accessing research materials, and training leaders. "All the Arts for All the Kids" is CAPP's slogan, and it embodies this philosophy by treating each of the arts—defined as dance, drama, creative writing, visual art, and music—as essential components of basic education. CAPP seeks to give school districts the tools for bringing arts education to all students in logical, sequential, and educationally sound programs.

Funding for CAPP comes from the Legislature and private sources, with school districts matching grant money. CAPP began with $125,000 in 1983. Now, state funding for the program is included in the $4.9 million legislative appropriation for the arts. Although this arrangement has brought CAPP a degree of stability, the program has not been totally shielded from budget cuts. A 20 percent cutback in the department of education's budget has reduced CAPP's allocation for the 1992-93 fiscal year to $38,000, compared to $76,000 during 1989-90 and $90,000 for 1986-87.

Budget cuts aside, CAPP enjoys widespread support, not only from state legislators, but also from the Minnesota State Arts Board, the state department of education, and the Minnesota Alliance for Arts in Education. These three organizations jointly administer CAPP through a public/private partnership. Local support is strengthened through leadership development programs and through district CAPP committees made up of parents, teachers, artists, and local business people.

The politics of inclusion brought the issue of arts education into educational discussions at many levels throughout the state, increasing the support for the arts in basic education. According to Sam Grabarski, executive director of the Minnesota State Arts Board, this broad-based support has been essential. "In many states, the arts are concentrated in the main metropolitan area. You don't get the public support because there's not a statewide interest." In Minnesota, though, CAPP combines statewide services with statewide support.

The Minnesota Center for Arts Education

The goal of the Minnesota Center for Arts Education, which was established through legislation in 1985, is to improve K-12 arts education statewide through outreach programs and a tuition-free residential arts high school. To serve more than a select group of talented students, the center offers opportunities to students, teachers, and artists throughout Minnesota through such initiatives as summer workshops, magnet programs, conferences, seminars, and publications. Because the center can bring together many disparate groups, it can encourage collaboration, discourage duplication of efforts, and stretch resources.

The Arts High School and Outcome-Based Education

The arts high school integrates concentrated training in the arts with study of general academic subjects. It also offers students an "outcome-based" education, an approach promoted throughout Minnesota that has increased the legitimacy of teaching the arts. Applying such a system to the arts—disciplines often considered "soft" or "insubstantial"—helps validate them by proving them to be measurable, solid, and productive.

Outcome-based education is defined in Minnesota's 1991 Education Omnibus Bill as a pupil-centered, results-oriented system in which
- what a pupil is to learn is clearly identified;
- each pupil's progress is based on demonstrated achievement;
- each pupil's needs are accommodated through multiple instructional strategies and assessment tools;
- each pupil is provided time and assistance to realize his or her potential.

Once the arts high school administrators chose an outcome-based system, they faced major decisions. What should students know, be able to do, value, and create? Before the administrators could assess outcomes, they had to decide what results they wanted to see.

The Arts and the Art of the Possible

Starting the Minnesota Center for Arts Education took time—and some compromises.

1985—The legislature establishes a school and resource center board and authorizes the resource center to begin operating in the 1985-86 school year.

1987—The legislature delays the start-up of the arts school until the fall of 1989 and changes it from a high school to a school for 11th and 12th grade students only.

1989—The legislature changes the name to the Minnesota Center for Arts Education. The school opens in rented facilities on the site of a former private college.

1990—The legislature authorizes the sale of bonds to purchase the college site.

1991—Further legislation clarifies that the Center is to operate a magnet program.

A lot of assessment in the arts high school is based on observation—especially when performance is measured. Many programs use portfolios, in which students collect samples of their work through the semester along with comments on their work. This system keeps students and teachers continually aware of progress, areas of concern, and the need for improvement, and it makes it difficult for teachers to let students "slip through the cracks."

As Barbara Martin, assistant director of the Minnesota Center for Arts Education, points out, "The arts have been taught this way for a long time, and this is the way professional artists assess their own work." She finds that what art teachers know about assessing work in the arts applies to general studies: There are outcomes that are compatible in science and in dance, in math and in theater, in language, and in social studies. Once identified, these similarities encourage dialogue between educators. Common goals provoke the collaboration that is the basis for the arts high school's interdisciplinary program.

Under current legislation, the school enrolls 11th and 12th grade students and offers one- and two-week seminars for students in the 9th and 10th grades

The Politics

The governor's office, the Minnesota Alliance for Arts in Education, and the Legislature have supported arts education in Minnesota. Even so, the road to comprehensive arts education has not been all straight and narrow, nor has progress always been fast.

The Minnesota Alliance for Arts in Education was the first group to enroll a lobbyist for arts education. It was also the only state alliance to insist on advocating arts in education rather than arts education. As Margaret

Haase, former chair of the alliance, has explained, "We weren't interested in 'art for art's sake.' We felt it was important to weave the arts into the general curriculum." So from the first, the alliance's long-range political platform has defined methods for infusing the arts into the school system.

Early in the 1980s, the alliance prepared an arts education plan for Minnesota. To advocate arts issues and strengthen personal relationships, the alliance in 1980 held a retreat for policymakers. It has also produced a handbook, *Working Together with Legislators and Public Officials*, that gives its political platform for the legislative session, lists the legislators involved in arts education initiatives, and advises people on how to support pending bills.

"The legislators are willing to put resources into high-quality programs that will reach students throughout the state," says Bill Marx, fiscal analyst with the House Ways and Means Committee. "Their concern is providing services to more than a select group of kids." The Legislature's support for arts education began with the passage of a bill in 1981 that directed the state department of education to report on the status of arts education in Minnesota public schools. After the report was complete, CAPP was implemented and pilot projects began throughout the state.

Evidence of legislators' support for arts education is the $4.9 million appropriated for the arts in 1985, which funded the Minnesota High School and Resource Center for the Arts, the CAPP program, and K-6 categorical aid for arts education. Though financial pressures have since brought some reductions in funding, Minnesota continues to back arts education strongly.

In Minnesota, the goal is comprehensive arts education, and the consensus seems to be in the Legislature and elsewhere that reaching this goal requires the investment of significant resources.

New Jersey: Toward Literacy in the Arts

In New Jersey, a single piece of legislation initiated a great deal of activity in arts education without applying burdensome regulation. By creating the Literacy in the Arts Task Force in 1987, New Jersey legislators gave arts advocates an opportunity to take an in-depth look at arts education in the public schools and to evaluate the state's commitment to arts education for all students. The work of the task force, in turn, spurred activities in schools. The result is a convincing demonstration that legislative initiative can lead to productive cooperation.

The Legislation

"The arts can offer all kids a place to succeed," concluded New Jersey Assemblywoman Maureen Ogden, legislator and ex-officio member of the State Arts Council. But, recognizing that legislation to strengthen arts education

Table 4
State Funding for Arts Education in Minnesota

A. Comprehensive Arts Planning Program (CAPP)

1983-85	$ 125,000 for biennium
1985-86	100,000
1986-87	90,000
1987-88	75,000
1988-89	75,000
1989-90	76,000
1990-91	76,000
1991-92	38,000
1992-93	38,000

B. Arts Education Aid (to all districts for elementary arts programs; $2.25 per student)

1985-86	$ 990,000
1986-87	990,000
1987-88	1,048,700

C. Categorical Reserve Arts Education Funding (set at 2.2 percent of the basic general education formula)

1986-87	$ 69.6 million
1987-88	75.7 million
1988-89	105.1 million
1989-90	120.4 million
1990-91	134.2 million

D. Minnesota Center for Arts Education

1985-86	$ 491,000
1986-87	2,037,000
1987-88	2,206,200
1988-89	2,649,500
1989-90	5,800,000 (school opens)
1990-91	5,875,000
1991-92	5,064,000
1992-93	5,057,000

could be difficult to pass without the support of the many groups it would affect, Assemblywoman Ogden sponsored a bill, with Senator Walter Rand, calling for the formation of a 25-member Literacy in the Arts Task Force. The Legislature appropriated $60,000 for the group and asked it to perform the following tasks:

- Study factors involved in providing sequential K-12 instruction in the arts;
- Develop a model K-12 curriculum for the performing and visual arts;
- Evaluate the effects of experience in the arts on the educational development of students;
- Survey all arts programs in the educational system and all other programs for exceptional students and make the results available to school districts;
- Explore the development of financial resources to support arts programs in the public schools;
- Study certification requirements for arts teachers and recommend changes to the state board of education.

The Task Force

Governor Thomas Kean asked Ernest L. Boyer, director of the Carnegie Foundation for the Advancement of Teaching, to chair the task force, and the members elected Carol Belt of the Alliance for Arts Education/NJ as vice chair. After first defining "the arts" as the visual arts, dance, theater, music, and creative writing (with more specific art forms such as photography or architecture defined as subcategories), task force members began looking at the condition of arts education in New Jersey. The results of their research were less than encouraging.

The task force found that, although state statutes and regulations strongly supported the arts, many children were receiving an unsatisfactory education in the arts. For example, while New Jersey had included the arts in its high school graduation requirements, the requirement could be satisfied with courses such as typing or auto mechanics. It was possible, concluded the task force, "for thousands of New Jersey's students to graduate each year without taking a single course in music, dance, theater, creative writing, or the visual arts."[1] A concentration on performance also concerned the task force, which felt that combining performance with the historical, aesthetic, interpretive, and critical aspects of the arts was essential to making students "literate." Students had only limited exposure to theater, dance, and the arts of non-Western cultures. Student/teacher ratios were too often high, facilities inappropriate, and materials and instruments in short supply. Assessment methods were inappropriate and inconsistent. It also became clear to the task force "that the arts will never be fully embraced if effective evaluation procedures are neglected."[2]

At the end of 18 months of study, the task force recommended that

- every school district in the state declare literacy in the arts a key educational objective for every student;
- every district develop a comprehensive program in all five art forms;
- all literacy in the arts programs include Western and non-Western cultures;

- all programs introduce students to the full range of the arts experience—as both senders and receivers;
- arts be taught "across the curriculum";
- arts education be fully accessible to all students, including the physically disabled and those with special learning needs;
- the classroom be extended to include museums, galleries, and theaters, and artists be engaged to work with teachers.[3]

The task force made some additional suggestions. It identified four developmental levels for K-12 students and discussed the activities appropriate to those levels. It outlined a model K-12 curriculum for arts education, forming a "framework" for each discipline at each developmental level. It recommended adding dance and creative writing to teacher certification categories, and it addressed assessment by asking educators and community groups to define core proficiencies for each of the arts.[4]

Calling funding "insufficient," the task force also made a series of recommendations about financing arts education. Because much of the money for arts programs in New Jersey is locally raised, it is vital that school districts be committed to the arts, and that state policymakers consider the real costs of the mandates they impose on districts.[5]

Among its specific recommendations to school districts, the task force included the notion that "school budgets include money to cover application and tuition fees for students who wish to attend specialized out-of-district arts education programs"[6] so that talented students can take advantage of opportunities that are already available. A specific recommendation to the Legislature was that it "include, in its educational appropriations, funds needed to help the education department and school districts implement the literacy and the arts imperative. . . . We also recommend that the state provide increased funding to the New Jersey State Council on the Arts in support of these initiatives."[7]

The task force also encouraged the Alliance for Arts Education/New Jersey to increase support for literacy in the arts and to coordinate arts education efforts.

A Progress Report

The Legislature has not appropriated much money for arts education, and New Jersey's current financial situation makes major appropriations unlikely in the near future. In 1987, the Legislature could have used the lack of financial resources as an excuse to avoid the issue of arts education. Yet Assemblywoman Ogden believed that "it was important to begin to get the 'arts as a basic discipline' message across to people," and doing at least that took no more than the $60,000 allocated to the Literacy in the Arts Task Force. From that beginning came considerable progress. The task force brought together all the groups in the state that are dedicated to arts education, and the resulting coalition is still at work. Rather than wait for more comprehensive legislation, funding, or mandates, the coalition took advantage of the visibility the task force gave arts education.

New Jersey has not suddenly found itself with a statewide, comprehensive arts education program as a result of this work, but many initiatives have since improved arts education programs and increased the number of stu-

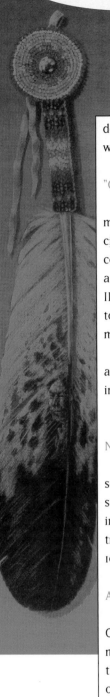

dents served by them. One significant improvement came when the department of education hired a specialist to work in the areas of arts education and gifted and talented programs.

"Core Course Proficiencies" and the Arts

In response to the task force's recommendation that the arts become part of basic education, the state department of education and the Alliance for Arts Education are incorporating the arts into the "core course proficiencies"—proficiencies students are expected to acquire in major subject areas. In English, for example, the core course proficiency outline, says "Vocabulary development should occur as an integral but natural consequence of a later activity—the study of literature, students' writing, fine arts, mythology, film, and so on. . . . In English I and II, activities might include viewing and discussing a play, a musical performance, a dance, and/or a series of photographs and reproductions of watercolors and oil paintings. . . . In experiencing and responding to non-print media, students must understand what they see. They must first learn the 'language' of the medium."[8]

The social studies core course proficiency outline includes the statement, "Students will analyze, interpret, create and use resources and materials which include. . .the arts, artifacts, and media. . . .[s]tudents will recognize the integral role of the arts as a vehicle of human expression, communication, and cultural identity."[9]

A separate core course proficiency for the arts was developed in 1992.

New Jersey School of the Arts

The New Jersey School of the Arts (NJSA) is a high school for talented New Jersey students. But the school's services are not limited to the students it accepts. The school's director, Abraham Beller, says that "a quality school for the arts stimulates arts throughout all schools in the state. It serves students not only with arts training, but with job training and college preparation." So, in 1991, for example, NJSA provided programs in 13 districts, six of which were incorporated into the regular school day. An "Urban Outreach Project" served more than 100 students, and 3,000 students attended NJSA workshops and career days.

Arts for Everykid

"Arts for Everykid" is a statewide campaign co-sponsored by the New Jersey Network, the New Jersey State Council on the Arts, and the Alliance for Arts Education to rally support for arts literacy for all students. The media portion of the campaign included a talk show/town meeting that was a forum for discussing such issues as the significance of the arts to education, the pertinence of arts education to children who are at risk of dropping out of school, and the challenge of financing comprehensive arts education in New Jersey. An hour-long documentary produced from the town meeting is already being shown on public television stations throughout the country. In addition, an advocacy handbook will be distributed throughout the state and nationally. Video-based workshops on advocacy and arts education are being conducted both for the educational community and the community at large. Support for the project was also provided by the National Endowment for the Arts. The three co-sponsors expect to continue the Arts for Everykid campaign at least through 1994.

The lesson to be learned from New Jersey's approach: Even minimal legislative support can be helpful if it is carefully thought out. Other states facing severe budget constraints may want to try creating a major task force for literacy in the arts. They would probably find, as New Jersey did, that their citizens and public organizations are fertile soil for the seeds of this type of policymaking.

Oklahoma: Arts Basic to Education

In Oklahoma, advocates for arts education are found at every level of education and policymaking. Legislative support for the arts is strong, witness the availability of state funds for arts education and the inclusion of the arts in Oklahoma's 1990 education reform bill. According to state Representative Sid Hudson, "The arts are not a 'program,' they're part of the basic curriculum just like any other subject. They've been considered basic for quite a while, and their inclusion in [the bill] simply confirms that position."

Legislative Support

Elsewhere, advocates of arts education often have to convince legislators that the arts are important to education. In Oklahoma, however, the lawmakers often educate the public on this point. Why? One reason is that in Oklahoma, a legislative caucus on the arts brings lawmakers together to discuss arts education and other issues in the arts. The group is bipartisan, and about 90 percent of the state's legislators participate.

The arts have been a line item in the education budget for ten years. Each year, $200,000 has been earmarked for teacher training and for improving arts programs in selected school districts. There has been little opposition to funding arts and culture both in and out of Oklahoma's schools. As state Senator Kelly Haney, an artist by profession, explains, investing in the arts pays off economically as well as culturally. "We conducted a study which showed that tax revenues from the arts come back at seven times the dollars we contribute to cultural events and tourism. That's quite significant."

The Education Reform and Funding Act of 1990

Among the arts organizations that formed a coalition to support House Bill 1017 were the Oklahoma Arts Institute, Individual Artists of Oklahoma, the Arts Council of Oklahoma City, and the University of Oklahoma Museum of Art. When they endorsed the bill, these groups

Education in the arts and humanities plays a central role in conveying our multi-cultural heritage, in developing the full potential of individuals, and in providing the basis for our living and working together as a democratic society.—Preamble to the 1991 Governor's Congress on the Arts and Humanities, Oklahoma.

emphasized the importance of the arts not just to creativity and self-esteem, but also to critical thinking and problem-solving. They also stressed the relevance of the arts to broad state interests. As the spokesperson for the coalition said, "When businesses and investors outside the state look at Oklahoma as a possible site for relocation or new industry, they consider many factors, including the quality of life. The condition of our education system and our cultural institutions are two major considerations."[10]

Oklahoma's Education Reform and Funding Act of 1990, which set new curriculum standards for public schools, mandated that students achieve competency in the following areas: math, science, arts, literature, languages, and social sciences. The inclusion of the arts in this list gives them a standing in the curriculum that they have in few other states. Placing them in the basic curriculum of the public schools secures them a line item in the general education budget and mandates the development of an assessment tool. For all these reasons, HB 1017 is having a strong effect on arts education in Oklahoma.

Arts in Basic Education

HB 1017 includes the arts in basic education in unambiguous terms. Section 6A reads, "By February 1, 1991, the State Board of Education shall adopt curricular standards for instruction of students in the public schools of this state that are to be implemented not later than the 1993-94 school year and that are necessary to ensure there is attainment of desired levels of competencies in a variety of areas to include language, social sciences, and communication. . . .Students, therefore, must study social sciences, literature, languages, the arts, mathematics, and science." The implementation of this curriculum is tied to accreditation. High schools must meet these standards by June 1995. Elementary and middle schools have until 1999.

An Interdisciplinary Approach

Initially, some schools and school districts assumed that including the arts in the curriculum would be expensive. But Oklahoma educators are learning that art can be infused into other academic subjects in ways that reduce expense and create good opportunities for interdisciplinary learning.

It is important to note that in Oklahoma, as in the other case-study states, the purpose of arts education is to teach students not simply how to make clay pots or give holiday concerts, but also to criticize, evaluate, perform, and appreciate art.

Learner Outcomes

Section 4.20 of HB 1017 addresses learner outcomes and the need for students to demonstrate competency in each academic subject. The department of education has responded by developing new learner outcomes for the fine arts. It has suggested outcomes for grades 1-12 in the visual arts and music and outcomes for grades 9-12 in drama/theater and dance.

The expectations for students in the arts are in accord with discipline-based arts education. Here, for example, are the expectations for visual art.

"Visual Art: As a result of instruction in Visual Art, students will be able to think, feel, and act creatively with visual art materials, acquire a knowledge of mankind's heritage of visual art and design, understand the nature of arts and the creative process, and more. Learner Outcomes are organized around four major instructional areas: aesthetics, art history, art criticism, and art production."[11]

Defining learner outcomes in this way has helped educators understand how to weave the arts into school schedules and budgets. As Sandy Garrett, state superintendent of schools, has pointed out, "The learner outcomes document endorsed by the state board of education. . . can be summarized in one sentence: Knowledge and skills come first, and there are many paths to achieving them. . . . Schools now have the opportunity to truly integrate the curriculum. Students can learn geography while they absorb history, read Shakespeare, or ponder science. . . Children can learn to read and write well. . . as a cast member in a school play."[12]

Assessing the Arts

HB 1017 requires that progress in the arts be assessed just as it is in other subjects: "Beginning with the 1992-93 school year, the board shall cause a criterion-referenced test to be administered to every student enrolled in the 12th grade of the public schools of this state. This test shall be designed to indicate whether competencies expected of Oklahoma high school graduates. . .have been mastered by the student. The test shall include sections on reading and writing of English, culture and the arts, mathematics. . . ."

Developing tests for the arts has proved more time-consuming and expensive than the Legislature hoped. Recognizing how important good assessment is to outcome-based education, the people in charge of testing in Oklahoma feel they cannot proceed until outcomes have been decided on and more money is available to develop assessment tools.

Governor's Congress on the Arts and Humanities

Every five years, the Oklahoma Governor's Congress on the Arts and Humanities, which first convened in 1986, gives hundreds of people an opportunity to address arts and humanities issues. The 1991 congress, which focused on education in the arts and humanities, resulted in the development of a state action plan.

Music Gains Status in Oklahoma

Students in Oklahoma will learn more about music than just how to make it. The department of education's new "learner outcomes" lay out high—and broad—expectations:

"Music: A generally educated music student is able to make music. . .create music, read music notation and will become acquainted with a wide variety of music styles. Students will develop listening skills and knowledge necessary to become intelligent consumers of music and more. Learner outcomes in general music are written in the categories of Performing/Reading, Creating, Listening/Describing and Valuing."

It is no understatement that the concept of the "arts as basic" is profound in its societal assumptions, revolutionary in its philosophy, (and) far reaching in its consequences—*ABC Plan.*

"Recognizing that HB 1017 mandates the inclusion of arts and humanities in grades K-12, we encourage implementation beyond minimal competency requirements in an inter-disciplinary and multi-cultural manner," reads one of the resolutions that came out of that plan, and it became the basis for a series of recommendations:

- All students in grades K-5 should have a "developmentally challenging arts curriculum."
- Students in higher grades should "be involved in arts and humanities activities" each year.
- Colleges and universities should make one year of education in the arts an admissions requirement.[13]

To these recommendations the Committee on Education and Training added others:

- Teacher education and certification programs should "promote infusion of the arts and humanities in an inter-disciplinary and multi-cultural manner."
- Teacher education programs should focus on the learner outcomes called for in HB 1017, and teacher examinations should refer to these outcomes.
- Practicing teachers should have opportunities for in-service training involving arts and humanities organizations, universities, and colleges.
- Funding should be sufficient to "ensure teachers achieve the competencies necessary to implement academic standards mandated by reform legislation."[14]

Multi-cultural Education

Oklahoma legislators want arts education to have a strong multi-cultural base, and they are expected to focus on multi-culturalism during their 1992 session. They may, for example, request that 12th-grade students be tested on the artistic contributions of various ethnic groups to American culture. These contributions exemplify a type of concrete subject matter in the arts that is often overlooked, and incorporating this kind of subject matter into the test would also acknowledge that the arts are natural tools for teaching multi-culturalism.

In sum, the arts, long a basic part of education in Oklahoma, are becoming ever more integrated into the education system—into the curriculum, into outcomes, into outcomes assessment. HB 1017 is an ambitious bill and one that can be expected to affect arts education in many ways for many years.

South Carolina: Arts in the Big Picture

When teachers and policymakers in South Carolina talk about ABC's, they're not talking about just reading, writing, and 'rithmetic. "ABC" in South Carolina also refers to the Arts in Basic Curriculum plan, the heart of this state's dedication to including arts in the public school curriculum.

South Carolina has been in the forefront of education reform since the passage of the omnibus Education

Improvement Act (EIA) of 1984. EIA concentrated on the basics of school improvement—the three R's, achievement scores, attendance rates—and addressed the arts in relation to programs for gifted and talented students. Target 2000, the state's 1989 school reform package, was a refinement of EIA and advanced beyond the basics. With this legislation, state policymakers demonstrated a commitment to comprehensive educational excellence, to pushing students beyond basic skills to critical thinking, creativity, and analysis.

The arts community, which was already developing a plan for arts education, saw a window of opportunity. Rather than competing with other disciplines, arts advocates joined forces with the education reformers. Result: the Arts in Basic Curriculum plan was incorporated into the Target 2000 legislation, and the arts became part of the big picture in South Carolina education.

Education Improvement Act

In an effort to reform a failing educational system, legislators in South Carolina, with strong leadership from former governor Richard Riley, passed the Education Improvement Act (EIA) in 1984 and funded it with a one-cent increase in the state sales tax. The legislation targeted eight areas: basic skills, elementary achievement, secondary achievement, SAT scores, student attendance, the number of high school graduates entering college, the number of vocational graduates employed in related fields, and the first-try pass rate on the exit exam.[15]

According to a 1986 report, What Is the Penny Buying for South Carolina?", the sales tax increase was being spent in the following ways: $7 million to schools for achievement gains and improved attendance; $195,704 in grants to teachers, and $32.9 million to build and repair schools or reduce millage rates. Only two years after the EIA passed, it seemed to be making a difference. Many new programs were being established for early childhood, remedial, vocational, and gifted and talented education. Student test scores were rising. Polls indicated that parents, teachers, and the public in general were pleased with the progress.[16]

Though the improvement continued, and the public continued to approve of the Education Improvement Act, legislators, educators, and business leaders were still concerned about educational excellence. In 1989, policymakers developed the second phase of South Carolina's education reform plan, Target 2000.

Target 2000

The goal of Target 2000, which passed in 1989, was to build on the EIA and to address such new issues as parental involvement, drop-out prevention, and programs for at-risk students. Perhaps most important for the arts, Target 2000 also aimed to move students forward from basic skills to higher-order thinking skills. In its final form, the legislation supported the ABC plan, mandating that students leave school able to demonstrate competence in the arts, among other subjects, and allocating $1.3 million for arts education.

Three factors contributed to the inclusion of the ABC initiatives in Target 2000. Because arts advocates had not waited for legislative action before developing a strategy for arts education, they were ready with the ABC plan when Target 2000 was taking shape. Because arts advocates had made an effort to educate legislators about the arts and education, inviting them to community events and organization meetings and finding out individual legislators' ties to the arts, the legislators were well informed about arts education. Rather than pitting themselves against science teachers, for example, or advocates of early-childhood education, arts educators allied themselves with educators from other disciplines when the time came to push for legislative support. As a result, Target 2000 incorporates the ABC initiatives.

ABC Plan

The work that led to the plan began in 1987 when the South Carolina Arts Commission used a grant from the National Endowment for the Arts to put together the ABC Steering Committee. The Commission set out to include all the major players—members of education organizations, arts organizations, and legislative committees, and also legislative staff. It invited a legislator, Representative Joseph H. Nesbitt (chair of the House Education Committee), to chair the steering committee.

Committee members shared two convictions: arts are basic to education and important to the quality of life in South Carolina and all children in the state's public schools should have equal opportunities to study the arts. In April 1988, the committee issued a report, "Plan for Arts in the Basic Curriculum" (see SIDEBAR).

The efforts of the steering committee and all the organizations it asked for support (the South Carolina Department of Education, the South Carolina Arts Commission, the South Carolina Alliance for Arts Education, among others) paid off in Target 2000 provisions that echo the steering committee's resolutions. For example,

Be It Resolved: The Arts are Basic

South Carolina's plan to incorporate the arts in basic education originated in these resolutions of the ABC Steering Committee:
· To define the arts as creative writing, dance, drama/theater, music, and visual arts;
· To establish curriculum guidelines that include appropriate emphases on creative expression, aesthetic perception, cultural heritage, and aesthetic valuing;
· To promote statewide endorsement of the arts curriculum frameworks developed by the department of education;
· To facilitate the development of curricula at the local level, sequenced grades K-12, within the parameters of state frameworks;
· To ensure the teaching of the arts by specialists for all students, and to promote the employment of district wide arts consultants/coordinators;
· To establish curriculum consultant positions addressing all arts disciplines at the department of education;
· To locate or develop model programs;
· To study the impact of requiring that at least one Carnegie Unit in one of the fine arts be required for high school graduation;
· To ensure that all four components of the state department of education's curriculum framework for the arts are integrated into the National Association of State Directors of Teacher Education and Certification (NASDTEC) program evaluation standards for teacher preparation programs in the arts;
· To create and implement generic and specialized service training "packages" for teachers generally and for teachers of the arts;
· To create an annual summer Arts Leadership Academy for selected teams of school administrators, teachers of the arts, and teacher educators in the arts;
· To create a long-range plan for teacher preparation and certification in dance and drama/theater and to conduct a feasibility study to assess appropriate preparation and certification in creative writing;
· To endorse the "Philadelphia Resolution" and "Concepts for Strengthening Arts Education in School" published by the Ad Hoc National Arts Education Working Group, March 24, 1986, and sponsored by the American Council for the Arts and the Music Educators National Conference;
· To develop a strong advocacy program to implement the ABC Plan resolutions.—ABC Steering Committee, *Plan for Arts in the Basic Curriculum.*

Target 2000 promotes the development of curricula in all four arts areas—visual arts, music, dance, and drama. It specifies that school districts use program funds to (1) develop and implement discipline-based arts education, (2) provide in-service training for arts specialists or classroom teachers, or (3) hire certified arts specialists or professional artists.

Pilot Projects

Target 2000 specifies a schedule, which runs from the 1989-90 school year through 1992-93, under which selected districts will pilot test the new arts education curricula before the curricula are introduced into all the schools in the state.

One pilot site is Pine Street Elementary School in Spartanburg, South Carolina. Educators here applied for a pilot grant "to restructure and revitalize our current programs while correlating them with new programs for all students in drama, dance, and creative writing."[17] Although the arts were already part of the educational experience for Pine Street students, involvement in ABC has allowed this school to broaden its offerings. Among the results so far: student time spent on dance has doubled, the relationship of the arts to other subjects has been strengthened, and educators have experimented with ways to build increased time for arts into the school day. Staff at Pine Street, like staff at other sites of pilot projects, will share their problems and successes with educators throughout the state.

Arts Curricula

Even before the ABC Steering Committee developed its plan, the department of education was creating curriculum frameworks for arts education. The visual arts framework was distributed to districts in 1985, and the music framework was published in 1988. One reason the department of education had made such progress: it employs two state arts consultants, one in music and one in visual arts.

The frameworks approach arts education as a separate discipline. The assumption is that students should learn aesthetic perception (awareness of aesthetic qualities), creative expression (the making of art), cultural heritage

The Language of ABC

The legislation mandating the Arts in Basic Curriculum Plan reads as follows:

"The state board of education, in conjunction with the S.C. Arts Commission, shall plan and develop discipline-based arts education curricula in the visual arts, music, dance, and drama which complies with the state department of education frameworks. The state department of education shall cause the arts education curricula to be pilot-tested in selected school districts during 1989-90, 1990-91, 1991-92, and 1992-93, and shall provide in-service training programs for arts specialists and classroom teachers. After pilot testing, the state department of education shall establish regulations related to in-service training and curriculum development in cooperation with the Arts in Basic Curriculum Steering Committee and after consultation with the Select Committee. These regulations shall encourage innovation and flexibility and reflect the integrity of instruction required by each arts discipline. These regulations must be developed in cooperation with school and district-level teachers and administrators. . . .

"The Joint Legislative Study Committee on Formula Funding shall review whether or not arts education should be given a weighting under the Education Finance Act. If appropriate, recommend a weighting, and report to the Select Committee by December 1, 1990. The General Assembly shall phase in the arts education program and funding for the arts education program after piloting over three years in substantially equal intervals."

(knowledge of the historical and cultural milieu in which art is created), and aesthetic valuing (development of critical thinking skills and ability to make informed judgments).

Having curriculum frameworks available proved a major advantage. The ABC Committee was able not only to present a sample framework to the legislature, but also to strengthen the claim that the arts are indeed "disciplines" worthy of being considered "basic" to the curriculum.

Higher Education

Many states have yet to forge adequate partnerships between educational institutions at all levels. But in South Carolina, higher education has played a part in reforming K-12 arts education.

Winthrop College, for example, has been deeply involved with the ABC project and has an ABC Project Office on campus. Winthrop has professional schools for education and the visual and performing arts, so one reason for its interest in ABC is an overall commitment to education and the arts. Another reason, according to Bennett Lentzner, dean of the School of Visual and Performing Arts, is that college programs in the arts depend on a supply of students who are literate in the arts, and those students come from the state's elementary and high schools. He cites yet another reason: "If we're going to make a difference in the world of arts, we've got to impact arts education. You make the citizenry literate in the arts by infusing the arts into the public school curriculum."

The Legislature

Lucky timing had a lot to do with the ABC Committee's success. But all the credit should not go to luck. Legislators in South Carolina were knowledgeable about the arts and considered the arts important. In fact, South Carolina is one of only a few states with a joint legislative committee on cultural affairs.

One source of legislative interest in the arts was doubtless the involvement of legislators and legislative staff on the ABC Steering Committee. Another possible influence is the interest of business and industry in arts and culture. South Carolina's Cultural Affairs Committee surveyed these constituents and found that "99 percent of the respondents indicated that they regard the arts as being important to the quality of life in the state."[18] Businesses demand good education in the communities where they locate, and business people have a sense that the arts are important to the quality of education.[19]

Lawmakers continue to show their support for arts education through their financial commitment to the ABC plan. Budget woes notwithstanding, South Carolina continues to increase its arts budget. Although some of the reasons for South Carolina's success in arts education are unique—the timing of Target 2000, the availability of arts specialists in the department of education, the legislature's record of support for the arts—other states could nonetheless learn from South Carolina's experience. One lesson is that good communication between arts advocates, educators, and legislators is a great asset. So is including members of all concerned groups in a planning effort like that of the ABC Steering Committee, because this strategy heads off possible conflicts.

A similar strategy of collaboration works well to push legislation, witness the successful alliance of arts advocates with educators in other disciplines. Perhaps most important, people who are concerned about arts education may need to take the initiative early, so that legislators can consider specific proposals, not just the general idea that the arts are important to education.

MOVING AHEAD TOGETHER

Improving education is never easy, as legislature after legislature has discovered, especially since the central action—more students learning more—is one that a legislature can only encourage, not mandate directly. Improving arts education is complicated by the many different people and groups who have a part to play; as we have seen, the impetus for change has come from sources as diverse as the federal government, school districts, and professional artists.

Collaboration has not always been the rule. But it is, as a rule, desirable. Ensuring the collaboration of the many groups that play a part in arts education is, therefore, a major possibility open to legislatures.

As Thomas Shannon, executive director of the National School Boards Association, has pointed out, the "arts education community" is bigger than legislators may at first realize. "It's a question of perspective. The makeup of the 'arts education community' has been defined too narrowly in the past. It is not composed just of those whose professional certification is in the field of arts education. It must include those school administrators and school board members who care about arts education and whose work affects what happens in arts education. Viewed in this broader, more inclusive context, the 'arts education community' has become a consortium of practitioners and advocates who hold educational administrative decisional authority and policymaking power."[1]

Adopting this "broader, more inclusive" view, let's look at major participants in arts education, at some of the challenges they confront, and then at the role legislatures can play in strengthening collaboration.

Major Participants

State Departments of Education

Though the relationships between legislatures and state departments of education are reasonably direct, a couple of factors complicate the ability of these departments to make the arts basic to education even where legislatures have mandated that result. In some cases, the departments do not have enough control over school districts to enforce legislative directives. In other cases, they are reluctant to push districts too hard.

As we have seen, South Carolina is a state in which the department of education has considerable control over school districts. There, the department mandates curriculum and sets standards. In a state like Colorado, however, school districts operate far more independently and often resist any "interference" from the state agency. Because the state constitution prohibits curriculum or testing mandates, the Colorado Department of Education cannot do a statewide assessment of the status of arts education, or collect statewide data.

Maine offers an example of a state department's reluctance to push for change where there is a sense that support for the arts is somewhat shaky. Even though the Maine Legislature passed a fine arts graduation requirement in 1984, the state department of education has been unwilling to come down too hard on districts that are not offering the arts. According to Sandra Long, the fine arts consultant at the Maine Department of Education, "The arts are still considered to be the fringes here, so if we push too hard, we may lose everything. We can't be too overt in pushing for the arts. An art teacher in every school is a goal and so are comprehensive arts programs. But there are no target dates."[2]

A further difficulty confronts departments of education that are trying to change arts education in the midst of changing many other aspects of education. Even though state departments typically employ arts curriculum specialists whose job it is to ensure that school districts carry out new laws and policies, those specialists often find it difficult to integrate changes in arts education with changes in other areas. Say that more site-based management is a tenet of education reform in a state that also seeks to strengthen the arts in basic education, then this combination of directives may seem incompatible and could leave a curriculum specialist wondering how to proceed, even with a strong state mandate.

Overcoming these problems would be difficult enough for departments of education in calmer times. But recent years have been far from calm in education. Whatever their resources in authority, money, and talent—and these vary widely from state to state—departments of education find themselves assailed by demands for reform on all sides. In many of them, arts education has been a low priority, and in every department it is only one of many responsibilities. Not surprisingly, this context complicates the job of the department and the job of arts groups that seek a department's support.

Higher Education

Though recent years have brought some interest in increasing collaboration between schools and colleges, advocates of arts education continue to find it difficult, if not impossible, to involve colleges and universities in making the arts basic to K-12 education. As many people have noted, there is usually little connection between fine arts departments and schools of education, a situation both caused by and resulting from the notion that the arts are only for the gifted.

South Carolina has shown that partnerships between higher education and elementary/secondary education can be productive; there, Winthrop College has the lead in overseeing South Carolina's art education program. According to South Carolina arts con-

"How can you make the citizenry literate in the arts? Infuse the arts into the public school curriculum. If that is to be done, then higher education needs to make a strong commitment to teacher education. If we're going to make a difference in the world of arts, we've got to impact arts education."
—Bennett Lintzer, President, Association of Fine Arts Deans

sultant MacArthur Goodwin, the time has come for arts advocates to turn their attention to higher education.

Also essential, according to Ronald Ross, director of the School of Music, University of Northern Iowa, are partnerships between arts educators and higher education administrators. At the University of Northern Iowa such a partnership recently produced a redefinition of how high school credits would be evaluated.

> "It sounds practical and hard-nosed to talk about cutting arts programs, but the school district doing that impoverishes its curriculum and cuts students off from some important—some basic—kinds of learning." —Albert Shanker, President, American Federation of Teachers

"Previously, students had been granted little credit for high-quality arts experiences," Ross says, "Several of us worked with university policymakers and admissions counselors to shape the revised standards to include a significant component of fine-arts course work. Such linkage of graduation requirements and admissions standards is crucial. It would be a hollow victory indeed if we succeeded in establishing more pervasive fine arts graduation requirements only to find our nation's colleges and universities unwilling to give proper acknowledgment to such work."[3]

If the arts are basic to elementary and secondary education, then perhaps they are also basic to higher education. This notion has received relatively little attention to date. But, as time goes on, other states are likely to follow the lead of Florida. There the advisory committee to ACE, Florida's "The Arts for a Complete Education" program, is working with higher education to mandate that students at Florida's public colleges and universities take at least one three-credit art course.

School Boards

There are more than 15,000 school boards across the nation, and gaining the support of their members is critical to the implementation of the comprehensive arts programs. Many boards adopt arts education as part of overall curriculum while others opt for the creation of a specific arts policy.

In 1990, the National School Boards Association (NSBA) passed a resolution urging its members to "establish and maintain comprehensive, multi-faceted arts education programs in their school districts." In a 1991 publication, *More than Pumpkins in October*, NSBA suggested first steps for boards to take:

"The impetus for a revised and expanded art education program may come from the grass roots up, from the top down, or even from outside your school system. However the realization of the need for such a program begins, the first steps toward its creation remain the same. Early on, your board discussions should deal with supervisory issues, curriculum creation or selection, and how best to communicate the changes to the public. Getting the process under way often requires a mix of boldness and patience."[4]

A knowledgeable arts supervisor who can direct the districts in curriculum matters is essential, NSBA points out. It recommends that supervisors oversee the K-12 art education program, not just coordinate the efforts of arts teachers.[5]

Principals

With the decentralization of school management, school administrators have gained authority for training, curriculum development, instruction, and scheduling. It follows that principals play a key leadership role in arts education.

The degree to which principals understand and appreciate arts education varies. Where principals have played an active role in arts education, they have given financial support for materials, found classroom space, and perhaps most important, seen that the arts are integrated into other subjects.

Arts Organizations

Through its Arts in Education program, the National Endowment for the Arts has helped state and local arts agencies work with education agencies on sequential programs in arts education. In fiscal year 1992 alone, state arts agencies received more than $5 million from the NEA to support arts education programs.
• Arts Education Partnership Grants go to state arts agencies to support artists in residence, teacher training, conferences, and development of the arts curriculum.
• Arts Plus is a pilot program to encourage arts agencies to work directly with schools or school districts to make the arts basic to all students.
• The Arts in Basic Education Grants, or AISBEG, has perhaps been NEA's most successful effort. It provides seed money and implementation funds for strategies that make the arts basic to education. The funds are given to arts agencies, which has forced cooperation between the arts community and state department of education. Though there was some initial resistance in the states, 33 states were participating in AISBEG by fiscal year 1990, and in most cases the result has been the formation of new partnerships.

State Arts Agencies

State arts agencies, which develop projects with local arts and cultural institutions, often view their chief educational function as making artists available to schools. These agencies also administer arts education grants, however, and offer technical assistance to schools. Each agency has an arts-in-education coordinator who administers the federal grants that are distributed to school districts.

These grants often serve as a springboard for legislative activity in the arts. In South Carolina, for example, it was the arts commission that drove the movement that ultimately led to legislation that will incorporate the arts into the basic curriculum. Sometimes, arts agencies develop joint projects with education agencies. In Utah, for example, the arts council worked with the Utah State Office of Education to develop exemplary arts-in-education programs in six schools. The hope is that the experience of the six schools will provide models for other schools to use.

Cultural Institutions

Museums, orchestras, and other cultural institutions provide invaluable first-hand experience in the arts. The trend is toward closer cooperation with schools. Museums, for example, are no longer simply a destination for the traditional field trip. Instead, they often send staff out to the schools to help teachers prepare students for visits. Many museums also send art exhibitions on tour so that students have a chance—often their first chance—to see art that they have studied in class. The excitement the children feel about the museum often carries over to the home.

"After a visit to the Sheldon Memorial Art Gallery in Lincoln, kids bring their parents back to educate them about art," says Sheila Brown, Nebraska Department of Education. "As a matter of fact, many of our students take their parents to museums on family vacations to other cities to visit famous art they learned about in class. Parents are frequently amazed at the depth of knowledge their children have about art."

Similarly, the National Dance Institute reaches out to school children so they can learn about ballet. Each year the institute sends professional dancers to four or five elementary schools to teach for the entire school year.

Increasingly, cultural institutions play a major role in promoting arts in education in the schools. By working with the teachers and in the schools, they are becoming extensions of the classroom.

The orchestra also creates free "orchestra primers" for teachers to use and sends docents into the schools to talk to students about the concerts they will attend. All told, the orchestra reaches 10,000 to 12,000 children each year.

Arts Alliances

In 1973, the John F. Kennedy Center for the Performing Arts and the U.S. Department of Education formed the Alliance for Arts Education. Now every state has an alliance committee whose purpose is to foster education in the arts for all students in all schools. Committee members are typically arts teachers, university and community arts leaders, artists, parents, other concerned citizens, and representatives of professional arts education associations, state departments of education, and state arts agencies. An arts alliance may host statewide conferences or develop resource guides for school districts. Alliances have also succeeded in implementing curriculum frameworks, perhaps because art teachers have helped to develop frameworks that schools and other art teachers are encouraged to adopt.

But probably more critical than an alliance's particular activities is its role as arts advocate. Take the arts

Bringing the "Classics" to Kids

The Colorado Springs Symphony Orchestra teaches future audiences to appreciate classical music. Each year it presents three "Adventure Series" concerts for children in a casual atmosphere on Saturday mornings. Funding comes from local arts groups and businesses. Last year, for example, the U.S. Space Foundation helped fund a program related to space exploration.

alliance in Minnesota, which has been one of the most active. According to Gene Merriam, senate finance chair, the Minnesota Alliance for Arts Education was the driving force behind the arts education movement and a leading proponent of education reform as well. By lobbying for programs and appropriations, providing services to schools and communities, and encouraging public awareness, it has been responsible for much of the legislative support that the arts have enjoyed in Minnesota. In other states, too, arts alliances have been essential to the passage of arts education legislation such as teacher certification for the arts, curriculum guidelines, and graduation requirements.

Obstacles to Cooperation

A few state arts agencies have had long, close relationships with their state departments of education. In Maine, for example, the arts agency was housed in the department of education for 17 years, though it has recently become a separate agency. In some states, education agencies and arts agencies have combined efforts to advocate change to the legislature. In general, though, collaboration has been the exception instead of the rule.

- Some arts agencies resist the idea of diverting money from the support of artists to the support of public education.
- Each type of agency tends to consider the other type of agency unwilling to cooperate.
- According to a survey recently published by the National Endowment for the Arts, many executive directors of arts agencies consider it inappropriate for them to take a leadership role in making the arts basic to education. Arts agencies should remain a resource for information on the arts, and maintain the artists in residence program, they say, and the push to make the arts basic to education should come from departments of education.[6]

Confirmation of this last difficulty comes from the NEA's AISBEG program, which requires arts and education agencies to cooperate. Many arts agencies report that they find it difficult to take the role of initiator with the education departments, especially in the area of curriculum development.

"Because these players often are called upon either to appear to or actually act in concert on arts education issues, their relationships with one another are critical to the success of arts education advocacy," says Anthony Radich, executive director, Missouri Arts Council. "Although they have long superficially shared the goal of making arts education more available, there are only a few examples of their working together effectively to attain this goal."

Even where state arts agencies might be willing to work closely with state departments of education, limitations on the influence of the education agency can limit the joint effort. In states like Wyoming or Colorado where the department of education has little control over school districts, the state arts agencies will in turn have little influ-

Arts Alliance as Catalyst

The Illinois Arts Alliance catalyzes change in the community and in the legislature. Its tactics: placing ads in newspapers, holding a rally in Chicago, producing a national public service announcement, distributing pre-printed postcards, putting out newsletters and action alerts.

The alliance works closely with state legislators to change the perception that the arts are expendable. Nadine Saitlin, director of the Illinois Alliance for Arts Education, encourages partnerships between the education and arts communities. "Our goal is to help prepare art professionals to deal with art education as part of the school improvement process and cultivate leadership in the development of local schools art programs."

ence on the educational system. Often, as Susan Witten, former arts consultant for the Ohio Department of Education, says school districts make their own choices:

"We don't say you have to teach these objectives, but we present leadership documents and tell every school district that they have to have a K-12 curriculum. We're there to try to enforce the standards, the minimums. We put a big effort into getting school districts to invite us to work with them. But, in the end, the districts are free to take it or leave it."[7]

The Legislature's Role: Encouraging Cooperation

No matter how difficult cooperation has been, in light of the fragmented responsibility for arts education and the differing viewpoints of major players, cooperation clearly works.

· The most successful initiatives have come in states like South Carolina, where the arts agency worked with the department of education during the education reform movement. Now the agency and the department are working together with higher education representatives to implement their Arts-in-Education plan, to develop the curriculum, and to determine assessment methods. "South Carolina is fairly unique in this arrangement," says Bennett Lentzner, fine arts dean, Winthrop College, "Higher education is not often involved anywhere in the country in these types of cooperative efforts."

· In Oklahoma, the scene was set for collaboration in arts education even before the onset of education reform. There, the Legislature has distributed money for arts education through the state department of education since 1970.

· In Kentucky, the development of a long-range plan for arts education is the result of cooperation by the Kentucky Arts Council, the board of education, and the Kentucky Alliance for Education, which jointly sponsored a series of regional hearings. One indication that cooperation is continuing through plan implementation: the arts council is helping the education board develop a comprehensive approach to in-service training of teachers.

· In Texas, the schools were understaffed and unable to comply with the 1983 legislative mandate to include the arts in the curriculum. Under the watch of the Legislature, the Texas Commission on the Arts and the Texas Education Agency entered into a partnership to develop the arts curriculum.

· Nebraska's Prairie Visions project, which the Nebraska Department of Education and the Nebraska Art Teachers Association originated, now has broad support from the Nebraska Alliance for Arts Education, the Nebraska Committee for the Humanities, the University of Nebraska, the Nebraska Council of School

Who's on First?

"It should not be our job to be the leader here, we are not the department of education," says Sam Grabarsky, executive director of the Minnesota Arts Board. Though Grabarsky thinks the board should use federal money to start projects, he maintains that the responsibility for arts education should then shift over to the department of education.

One problem may be that the goals of the two agencies at first seem incompatible. Another factor: differences in political power. Arts agencies simply do not make the financial demands on legislatures that education departments do, nor carry the political clout. In New York, for example, where the department of education is the largest state agency, the budget for K-12 education was $9.6 billion for FY 1992, whereas the New York Council on the Arts received $32 million.

Administrators, and more than 50 school districts. Furthermore, four regional museums offer lectures for teachers and demonstrations of how teachers can use museums as extensions of their classrooms. "We are constantly reaching out to find new partners in arts education," says coordinator Sheila Brown. "That's the real success of our program."

It's perfectly possible for collaboration to be voluntary. According to the NEA survey, for example, most arts specialists in departments of education want to collaborate with the arts organizations and advocates such as the arts alliances. But very often, collaboration has required legislative involvement.

• In New Jersey, it was a sense of shared adversity—the 1987 announcement by the state school board that it planned to eliminate the arts graduation requirement—that originally drew the arts community and the education community together. The arts community subsequently took its cause to the Legislature and the requirement was reinstated.

• In 1984 the Utah Legislature set the stage for cooperation by setting up a model site program under the arts council, but awarding the $140,000 that funded the program to the office of education. Although there were spirited debates about how to best implement the program, the Legislature wound up forcing the two groups to collaborate. The program was an eventual success.

• Florida's ACE program, "The Arts for a Complete Education," was started with a planning grant from the NEA and $500,000 in state matching funds. To ensure cooperation, the Legislature split the appropriation between the Division of Cultural Affairs and the department of education. The goal: make the arts part of the basic curriculum from prekindergarten through college.

One researcher sums it up by saying, "This issue of translating state bills and acts into reality, by using a kid-glove approach and by keeping a gentle pressure on during uneven economic times, is what finally has brought departments of education to the sometimes wary, sometimes uncomfortable, but intensely necessary partnership with state arts agencies."[8] The unstated corollary is that it is often the state legislature (and sometimes only the state legislature) that is in a position to encourage, or even force, collaboration where it is as intensely resisted as it is intensely necessary.

As state legislators become deeply involved in education reform, they are reassessing their proper role. Many legislators have come to the conclusion

Collaboration in Missouri

The Missouri Arts Council made the Missouri Department of Education an offer it couldn't refuse. By offering to share the cost of funding an arts specialist at the department of education, the arts council was able to assist in the development of curriculum guidelines and oversee district programs. In fiscal year 1990 the arts council provided $12,500 and leveraged an additional $12,500 from the NEA, and the department of education used a $25,000 appropriation from the legislature. The arts council and department will share funding for the next four years and then the legislature will fully fund the position.

"It's about the only way that the arts could get onto the education agenda," says Representative Sheila Lumpe, a member of the Missouri Arts Education Task Force. "The arts have an uphill battle in that they are competing for the same educational dollar as math and science. It's not fair, but that's reality." Lumpe says that the main responsibility for advocating the arts in education lies with the arts councils. She credits advocacy groups with pushing the legislature to recognize the educational advantages of including the arts in education. "Many school administrators, parents, and teachers don't value the arts," says Lumpe. "So it's not surprising that the legislature doesn't get it. There was a really big selling job on the part of arts advocates to show the connection between the arts and math and science."

Anthony Radich, director of the Missouri Arts Council, agrees. Because education agencies respond to what's topical—math, science, sports—the arts councils need to take a leadership role in the development of arts education policy. Says Radich, "If we are going to be successful, we have to be inclusive in all arts endeavors. We can't survive if we fund only artists and ignore what's going on in the schools."

that it is time to stop micro-managing education, time instead to set broad goals for education and empower schools to meet them. This means asking what students should be able to know and do when they leave school rather than asking them to answer pre-determined questions on a standardized test. It means encouraging cooperation between arts advocates and education agencies rather than dictating their every move. "This asks a lot of legislative restraint," says Representative Ken Nelson, chair of the Minnesota House Education Finance Committee. "Our challenge is to back off and let those who are closest to the students decide what's best."

A second conclusion seems just as broadly valid: arts education is not another "special-interest" program in search of special funding, but an integral part of education. David O'Fallon, director of the Kennedy Centers' Education Department, and former director of the NEA Arts in Education program, summed up this point: "We are not asking the schools to add one more class to the required curriculum. If they added everything that education advocates asked for, the school day would be 18 hours long! Rather, we are presenting the arts to the schools as a way to help them prepare students to enter college and, ultimately, the workforce."

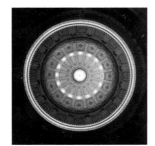

STATE CONTACTS

ALABAMA
Alabama State Council on the Arts and
Humanities
One Dexter Avenue
Montgomery, Alabama 36130
(205) 242-4076
(205) 240-3269 (FAX)

Music Education Specialist
Visual Arts Specialist
Alabama Department of Education
Gordon Persons Office Building
50 N. Ripley Street
Montgomery, Alabama 36130-3901
(205) 242-9700

ALASKA
Alaska State Council on the Arts
411 W. 4th Avenue, Suite 1E
Anchorage, Alaska
(907) 276-1558
(907) 279-4330 (FAX)

Curriculum Specialist
Language Arts/Fine Arts
Alaska Department of Education
Goldbelt Building
P.O. Box F
Juneau, Alaska 99811
(907) 465-2800

ARIZONA
Arizona Commission on the Arts
417 W. Roosevelt Avenue
Phoenix, Arizona 85003
(602) 255-5882
(207) 256-0282 (FAX)

Performing Arts Specialist
Visual Arts Specialist
State Department of Education
1535 W. Jefferson
Phoenix, Arizona 85007
(602) 542-4361

ARKANSAS
Arkansas Arts Council
Heritage Center
225 E. Markham, Suite 200
Little Rock, Arkansas 72201
(501) 324-9337
(501) 324-9345 (FAX)

Art Education Specialist
Music Education Specialist

Arkansas Department of Education
Four State Capitol Mall
Room 304A
Little Rock, Arkansas 72201-1071
(501) 682-4204

CALIFORNIA
California Arts Council
2411 Alhambra Boulevard
Sacramento, California 95817
(916) 739-3186
(916) 739-5008 (FAX)

Arts Consultant
Social Studies/Fine Arts
California Department of Education
P.O. Box 944272
721 Capitol Mall
Sacramento, California 95814
(916) 657-5485

COLORADO
Colorado Council on the Arts
and Humanities
Grant-Humphreys Mansion
750 Pennsylvania Street
Denver, Colorado 80203
(303) 894-2617
(303) 894-2615 (FAX)

Fine Arts Consultant
Colorado Department of Education
201 E. Colfax Avenue
Denver, Colorado 80203-1705
(303) 866-6600

CONNECTICUT
Connecticut Commission on the Arts
227 Lawrence Street
Hartford, Connecticut 06106
(203) 566-4770
(203) 566-6462 (FAX)

Art Education Consultant
Music Education Consultant
Connecticut Department of Education
165 Capitol Avenue
State Office Building
Hartford, Connecticut 06106-1630
(203) 566-5061

DELAWARE
Delaware State Arts Council
State Office Building
820 N. French Street
Wilmington, Delaware 19801
(302) 577-3540
(302) 577-3862 (FAX)

State Department of Public
Information
P.O. Box 1402
Townsend Building, #279
Dover, Delaware 19903
(302) 739-4601

DISTRICT OF COLUMBIA
D.C. Commission on the Arts and
Humanities
410 8th Street NW, 5th Floor
Washington, D.C. 20004
(202) 724-5613
(202) 727-4135 (FAX)

Curriculum Director of Art
Curriculum Director of Music
District of Columbia Public Schools
The Presidential Building
415 12th Street N.W.
Washington, D.C. 20004
(202) 724-4222

FLORIDA
Division of Cultural Affairs
The Capitol
Tallahassee, Florida 32399-0250
(904) 487-2980
(904) 922-5259 (FAX)

Art Specialist
Dance Specialist
Music and Drama Specialist
State Department of Education
Capitol Building, Room PL 08
Tallahassee, Florida 32301
(904) 487-1785

GEORGIA
Georgia Council for the Arts and
Humanities
530 Means Street NW, Suite 115
Atlanta, Georgia 30318
(404) 651-7920
(404) 651-7922 (FAX)

Coordinator, Fine Arts
Music Consultant
Georgia Department of Education
2066 Twin Towers East
205 Butler Street
Atlanta, Georgia 30334
(404) 656-2800

Consultant, Dance
Georgia Department of Health
1960 Twin Towers East
Atlanta, Georgia 30334-5040

HAWAII
State Foundation on Culture and The
Arts
c/o 189 Lunalilo Home Road
Honolulu, Hawaii 96825
(808) 396-2534

Arts Education Specialist
Educational Specialist
Fine Arts Specialist
Music Specialist II
Department of Education
1390 Miller Street
Honolulu, Hawaii 96813
(808) 586-3310

IDAHO
Idaho Commission on the Arts
304 W. State Street
Boise, Idaho 83720
(208) 334-2119
(208) 334-2488 (FAX)

Consultant, Fine Arts
State Department of Education
Len B. Jordan Office Building
650 W. State Street
Boise, Idaho 83720
(208) 334-2270

ILLINOIS
Illinois Arts Council
State of Illinois Center
100 W. Randolph Street, Suite 10-500
Chicago, Illinois 60601
(312) 814-6750
(312) 814-1471 (FAX)

Assessment Specialist
Illinois State Board of Education
100 N. First Street
Springfield, Illinois 62777
(217) 782-2221

INDIANA

Indiana Arts Commission
Indiana Government Center South
402 W. Washington Street, Room 072
Indianapolis, Indiana 46204-2741
(317) 232-1268
(317) 232-5595 (FAX)

Arts Consultant
Indiana Department of Education
Room 229, State House
100 N. Capitol Street
Indianapolis, Indiana 46204
(317) 232-6665

IOWA

Iowa Arts Council
Capitol Complex
Des Moines, Iowa 50319
(515) 281-4451
(515) 242-6498 (FAX)

State Department of Education
Grimes State Office Building
East 14th and Grand Streets
Des Moines, Iowa 50319-0146
(515) 281-5294

KANSAS

Kansas Arts Commission
Jayhawk Towers, Suite 1004
700 Jackson
Topeka, Kansas 66603
(913) 296-3335
(913) 296-4090 (FAX)

Education Program Specialist
Kansas State Department of Education
120 E. Tenth Street
Topeka, Kansas 66612-1182
(913) 296-3202

KENTUCKY

Kentucky Arts Council
31 Fountain Place
Frankfort, Kentucky 40601-1942
(502) 564-3757
(502) 564-2839 (FAX)

Director, Unit for Arts
1824 Capitol Plaza Tower
Frankfort, Kentucky 40601
Consultant, Music Education
Visual Arts Consultant
Kentucky Department of Education
Capitol Plaza Tower
500 Mero Street
Frankfort, Kentucky 40601
(502) 564-4770

LOUISIANA

Department of Culture, Recreation,
and Tourism, Division of the Arts
1051 N. 3rd Street, P.O. Box 44247
Baton Rouge, Louisiana
(504) 342-8180
(504) 342-3207 (FAX)

Arts and Humanities Supervisor
Music Education Supervisor
Louisiana Department of Education
P.O. Box 94064, 626 N. 4th Street
12th Floor
Baton Rouge, Louisiana 70804-9064
(504) 342-3602

MAINE

Maine Arts Commission
55 Capitol Street
State House Station 25
Augusta, Maine 04333
(207) 289-2724
(207) 289-2861 (FAX - Tourism Dept.)

State Department of Education
State House Station No. 23
Augusta, Maine 04333
(207) 289-5800

MARYLAND

Maryland State Arts Council
15 W. Mulberry Street
Baltimore, Maryland 21201
(410) 333-8232
(410) 333-1062 (FAX)

Arts and Humanities Section
Maryland Department of Education
200 W. Baltimore Street
Baltimore, Maryland 21201
(410) 333-2200

MASSACHUSETTS

Massachusetts Cultural Council
80 Boylston Street
The Little Building, 10th Floor
Boston, Massachusetts 02116
(617) 727-3668
(617) 727-0044 (FAX)

State Department of Education
Quincy Center Plaza
1385 Hancock Street
Quincy, Massachusetts 02169
(617) 770-7321

MICHIGAN

Michigan Council for the Arts and
Cultural Affairs
1200 Sixth Avenue
Executive Plaza
Detroit, Michigan 48226-2461
(313) 256-3735
(313) 256-3781 (FAX)

Arts Education Specialist
Michigan Department of Education
P.O. Box 30008
608 W. Allegan Street
Lansing, Michigan 48909
(517) 373-3354

MINNESOTA

Minnesota State Arts Board
432 Summit Avenue
St. Paul, Minnesota 55102
(612) 297-2603
(612) 297-4304 (FAX)

Dance Specialist
Theater Specialist
Minnesota Department of Education
629 Capitol Square Building
St. Paul, Minnesota 55101
(612) 296-2358

MISSISSIPPI

Mississippi Arts Commission
239 N. Lamar Street, Suite 207
Jackson, Mississippi 39201-1311
(601) 359-6030
(601) 359-1500 (FAX)

Music Education Consultant
Mississippi Department of Education
P.O. Box 771
550 High Street, Room 501
Jackson, Mississippi 39205-0771
(601) 359-3513

MISSOURI

Missouri State Council on the Arts
560 Trinity Avenue
St. Louis, Missouri 63130
(314) 727-4422

Coordinator of Curriculum
Missouri Department of Education
P.O. Box 480
205 Jefferson Street, 6th Floor
Jefferson City, Missouri 65102
(314) 751-4446

MONTANA

Montana Arts Council
316 N. Park Avenue, Room 252
Helena, Montana 59620
(406) 447-8390

Curriculum Manager
Montana Office of Public Instruction
106 State Capitol
Helena, Montana 59620
(406) 444-3680

NEBRASKA

Nebraska Arts Council
1313 Farnam-on-the-Mall
Omaha, Nebraska 68102-1873
(402) 896-3771
(402) 595-2217 (FAX)

Fine Arts Consultant
Nebraska Department of Education
301 Centennial Mall, South
P.O. Box 94987
Lincoln, Nebraska 68509
(402) 471-5020

NEVADA

Nevada State Council on the Arts
329 Flint Street
Reno, Nevada 89501
(702) 688-1225
(702) 688-1110 (FAX)

State Department of Education
Capitol Complex
400 W. King Street
Carson City, Nevada 89710
(702) 687-3100

NEW HAMPSHIRE
New Hampshire State Council on the Arts
Phoenix Hall
40 N. Main Street
Concord, New Hampshire 03301
(603) 271-2789

New Hampshire Department of
Education
101 Pleasant Street
State Office Park South
Concord, New Hampshire 03301
(603) 271-3144
(314) 727-5746 (FAX)

NEW JERSEY
New Jersey State Council on the Arts
4 N. Broad Street, CN 306
Trenton, New Jersey 08625
(609) 292-6130
(609) 984-7018
(609) 989-1440 (FAX)

Department of Education
225 W. State Street, CN 500
Trenton, New Jersey 08625-0500
(609) 292-4450
(314) 727-5746 (FAX)

NEW MEXICO
New Mexico Arts Division
224 E. Palace Avenue
Santa Fe, New Mexico 87501
(505) 827-6490
(505) 827-7308 (FAX)

Art Education Specialist
Music Education and Theater
State Department of Education
Education Building
300 Don Gaspar
Santa Fe, New Mexico 87501-2786
(505) 827-6516
(505) 727-5746 (FAX)

NEW YORK
Associate in Arts Education
New York State Council on the Arts
915 Broadway
New York, New York 10010
(212) 387-7139
(212) 387-7164 (FAX)

New York Foundation for the Arts
5 Beekman Street, Suite 600
New York, New York 10038
(212) 233-3900

NORTH CAROLINA
North Carolina Arts Council
Department of Cultural Resources
Raleigh, North Carolina 27601-2801
(919) 733-7897
(919) 733-4834 (FAX)

Arts Education Section
North Carolina Department of Public
Instruction
Education Building
116 W. Edenton Street
Raleigh, North Carolina 27603-1712
(919) 733-3813

NORTH DAKOTA
North Dakota Council on the Arts
118 Broadway
Black Building, Suite 606
Fargo, North Dakota 58102-0788
(701) 239-7150
(701) 239-7153 (FAX)

Director of Curriculum
North Dakota Department of Public
Instruction
State Capitol Building, 11th Floor
600 Boulevard Avenue East
Bismarck, North Dakota 58505-0440
(701) 224-2261

OHIO
Ohio Arts Council
727 E. Main Street
Columbus, Ohio 43205
(614) 466-2613
(614) 466-4494 (FAX)

Art Education Consultant
Music Education Consultant
Physical Education Consultant
Ohio Department of Education
65 S. Front Street, Room 808
Columbus, Ohio 43266-0308
(614) 466-3304

OKLAHOMA
State Arts Council of Oklahoma
Jim Thorpe Building, Room 640
2101 N. Lincoln Boulevard
Oklahoma City, Oklahoma 73105
(405) 521-2931
(405) 521-6418 (FAX)

Coordinator, Arts in Education
Oklahoma Department of Education
Hodge Education Building
2500 N. Lincoln Boulevard
Oklahoma City, Oklahoma 73105-4599
(405) 521-3301

OREGON
Oregon Arts Commission
550 Airport Road
Salem, Oregon
(503) 378-3625
(503) 373-7789 (FAX)

English Language Arts Specialist
Music Education Specialist
Physical Education Specialist
Visual Arts Education Specialist
Oregon Department of Education
700 Pringle Parkway SE
Salem, Oregon 93710
(503) 378-3573

PENNSYLVANIA
Pennsylvania Council on the Arts
Room 216, Finance Building
Harrisburg, Pennsylvania 17120
(717) 787-6883
(717) 787-8614 (FAX)

Arts Advisor
Pennsylvania Department of Education
333 Market Street, 10th Floor
Harrisburg, Pennsylvania 17126-0333
(717) 787-5820

RHODE ISLAND
Rhode Island State Council on the Arts
95 Cedar Street, Suite 103
Providence, Rhode Island 02903
(401) 277-3880

Arts Consultant
Rhode Island Department of Education
22 Hayes Street
Providence, Rhode Island 02908
(401) 277-2617

SOUTH CAROLINA
South Carolina Arts Commission
1800 Gervais Street
Columbia, South Carolina 29201-3585
(803) 734-8696
(803) 734-8526 (FAX)

Art Consultant
Music Consultant
South Carolina Department of
Education
1429 Senate Street
Columbia, South Carolina 29201
(803) 734-8492

SOUTH DAKOTA
South Dakota Arts Council
230 S. Phillips Avenue, Suite 204
Sioux Falls, South Dakota 57102-0720
(605) 339-6646
(605) 32-7965 (FAX)

Education and Cultural Affairs
700 Governors Drive
Pierre, South Dakota 57501-2291
(605) 773-3134

TENNESSEE
Tennessee Arts Commission
320 Sixth Avenue N., Suite 100
Nashville, Tennessee 37243-0780
(615) 741-6395
(615) 741-58290 c/o Bob Benson; Film,
Tape, & Music Commission (FAX)

Arts Education
Art Consultant
Music Consultant
State Department of Education
100 Cordell Hull Building
Nashville, Tennessee 37219
(615) 741-2731

TEXAS
Texas Commission on the Arts
P.O. Box 13406, Capitol Station
Austin, Texas 78711
(512) 463-5535
(512) 475-2699 (FAX)

Art Specialist
Fine Arts/Music Specialist
Theater Specialist
Texas Education Agency
William B. Travis Building
1701 N. Congress Avenue
Austin, Texas 78701-1494
(512) 463-8985

UTAH
Utah Arts Council
617 East South Temple Street
Salt Lake City, Utah 84102
(801) 533-5895
(801) 533-6196 (FAX)

Art Education Specialist
State Office of Education
250 East 500 South
Salt Lake City, Utah 84111
(801) 538-7510

VERMONT
Vermont Council On The Arts, Inc.
136 State Street
Montpelier, Vermont 05602
(802) 828-3291
(802) 828-3233 (FAX)

Arts Consultant
State Department of Education
120 State Street
Montpelier, Vermont 05602-2703
(802) 828-3135

VIRGINIA
Vermont Commission For The Arts
Lewis House - 2nd Floor
223 Governor Street
Richmond, Virginia 23219-2010
(804) 225-3132
(804) 225-4327 (FAX)

Supervisor of English
Supervisor of Music
Very Special Arts
Department of Education
P. O. Box 6-Q, James Monroe Building
Fourteenth and Franklin Streets
Richmond, Virginia 23216-2060
(804) 225-2755

WASHINGTON
Washington State Arts Commission
9th and Columbia Building
P.O. Box 42675
Olympia, Washington 98504-4111
(206) 753-3860
(206) 586-5351 (FAX)

Superintendent of Public Instruction
Old Capitol Building
P.O. Box 47200
Washington and Legion
Olympia, Washington 98504-7200

(206) 586-6904

WEST VIRGINIA
Arts Representative
Cultural Center
Arts and Humanities Section
Capitol Complex
Charleston, West Virginia 25305
(304) 348-0240
(304) 348-2779 (FAX)

Coordinator, Fine Arts
West Virginia Department of Education
1900 Kanawha Boulevard, East
Building 6, Room B-358
Charleston, West Virginia 25305
(304) 348-2681

WISCONSIN
Wisconsin Arts Board
131 W. Wilson Street, Suite 301
Madison, Wisconsin 53702
(608) 266-0190
(608) 267-0380 (FAX)

Language Arts Consultant
Music Consultant
Visual Art Consultant
Department of Public Instruction
General Executive Facility 3
125 S. Webster Street
P. O. Box 7841
Madison, Wisconsin 53707
(608) 266-1771

WYOMING
Wyoming Council on the Arts
2320 Capitol Avenue
Cheyenne, Wyoming 82002
(307) 777-7742
(307) 777-5499 (FAX)

Education Program Specialist
State Department of Education
2300 Capitol Avenue, 2nd Floor
Hathaway Building
Cheyenne, Wyoming 82002-0050
(307) 777-7675

AMERICAN SAMOA
Arts in Education Coordinator
Office of the Governor
P.O. Box 1540
Pago Pago, Tutuila 96799
011 (684) 633-4347

Teacher Certification and
Staff Development Office
Department of Education
Pago Pago, Tutuila 96799
011 (684) 633-5237

NATIONAL CONTACTS

Adjunct ERIC Clearinghouse for Art
Education
Indiana University
Social Studies Development Center
2805 E. 10th Street, Suite 120
Bloomington, Indiana 47408
(812) 855-3838

American Council for the Arts
1285 Avenue of the Americas
3rd Floor, Area M
New York, New York 10019
(212) 245-4510

Council of Chief State School Officers
One Massachusetts Avenue NW,
Suite 700
Washington, D.C. 20001
(202) 408-5505

DANCE/USA
777 14th Street NW, Suite 540
Washington, D.C. 20005
(202) 628-0144

Educational Theater Association
3368 Central Parkway
Cincinnati, Ohio 45225
(513) 599-1996

Getty Center for Education in the Arts
401 Wilshire Boulevard, Suite 950
Santa Monica, California 90401
(310) 395-6657

John F. Kennedy Center for the
Performing Arts
Education Department
Washington, D.C. 20566
(202) 416-8800

Music Educators National Conference
1902 Association Drive
Reston, Virginia 22091

National Assembly of State Arts
Agencies
1010 Vermont Avenue NW, Suite 920
Washington, D.C. 20005

(202) 347-6352
National Art Education Association
1916 Association Drive
Reston, Virginia 22091
(703) 860-8000

National Arts Education Research
Center
New York University
26 Washington Place, Room 21
New York, New York 10003
(212) 998-6050

National Dance Association
1900 Association Drive
Reston, Virginia 22091
(703) 476-3436

National Endowment for the Arts
Division of Education Programs or
Museums and Historical Organizations
Program
1100 Pennsylvania Avenue NW
Washington, D.C. 20506

National Endowment for the
Humanities
Division of Education Programs or
Museums and Historical Organizations
Program
1100 Pennsylvania Avenue NW
Washington, D.C. 20506
(202) 786-0438

National Parent Teacher Association
Publications Department
700 N. Rush Street
Chicago, Illinois 60611
(312) 787-0977

National School Boards Association
1680 Duke Street
Alexandria, Virginia 22314
(703) 838-6722

INTRODUCTION

1. Louis Harris, *Americans and the Arts VI: Highlights from a Nationwide Survey of Public Opinion* (New York, N.Y.: American Council on the Arts, 1992).

PART I

1. National Commission on Excellence in Education, *A Nation at Risk: The Imperative for Education Reform* (Washington, D.C., April 1983), p. 3.
2. Howard Gardner, *Frames of Mind: The Theory of Multiple Intelligences* (New York, N.Y.: Basic Books, 1983), p.2.
3. The College Board, *Academic Preparation for College: What Students Need to Know and Be Able to Do* (New York, N.Y., 1983), pp. 16-18.
4. Judith Hanna, *Connections: Arts, Academics, and Productive Citizens* 73 (Phi Delta Kappan, April 1992): p. 603.
5. National School Boards Association, *More than Pumpkins in October: Visual Literacy in the 21st Century* (Washington, D.C., December 1990), p. 33.
6. Ellyn Berk and Jerrold Ross, *Principal Research Findings 1987-1991* (New York: National Arts Education Research Center, New York University,n.d.), p. 1.
7. Ibid.
8. Ibid., p. 2.
9. Music Educators National Conference et al., "K-12 Arts Education in the United States: Present Context, Future Needs, A Briefing Paper for the Arts Education Community" (Reston, Va., January 1986).
10. Miriam Horn, "Looking for a Renaissance: The Campaign to Revive Education in the Arts" (*U.S. News and World Report*, March 30, 1992), p. 54.
11. Judith Hanna, "Using the Arts as a Dropout Prevention Tool," *The Brown University Child Behavior and Development Letter* 7 (March 1991): 3.
12. Ellyn Berk, ed., *A Framework for Multicultural Arts* (New York, N.Y.: National Arts Education Research Center, 1991), p. 1.
13. Ibid., p. 2.
14. Hanna, *Connections*, p. 601.
15. National School Boards Association, *More than Pumpkins in October*, p. 45.

PART II

1. U.S. Department of Education et al., *Estimates of School Statistics*, 1990-91.
2. Ibid.
3. State Higher Education Executive Officers, *State Appropriations for Higher Education 1991-92* (Denver, Colo., April 1992).

PART III

1. National Board for Professional Teaching Standards, *What Teachers Should Know and Be Able to Do* (Washington, D.C., n.d.), p. 13.
2. Robert Glidden, "The K-12 Arts Agenda: Next Challenges for Higher Education," *Design for Arts in Education*, September/October 1989, p. 11.
3. "Teacher Education Update," *Chronicle of Higher Education*, October 30, 1991, p. 20.
4. Marilyn Price-Richard, *Art Education: Certification and Teacher Education*, A Report on Research for the Getty Center for Education in the Arts (Los Angeles, Calif., December 1989).
5. Charles Dorn, "The Florida State Initial Teacher Certification Test: A Case Study," *Design for Arts Education*, March/April 1989, p. 37.
6. Kathryn Martin and Jerrold Ross, "Developing Professionals for Arts Education" in *Toward a New Era in Arts Education*, ed. John T. McLaughlin (New York, N.Y.: American Council for the Arts, 1988), p. 38.
7. Jonathan Katz, *Arts Education Handbook: A Guide to Productive Collaborations* (Washington, D.C.: National Assembly of State Arts Agencies, 1988), p. 19.
8. Ibid., pp. 78-79.
9. "Tennessee Requires Fine Arts for University Admission," *NAEA News* No 2, Reston, Va., 31 (April 1990): 1.
10. Paul Lehman and Richard Sinatra, *Assessing Arts Curricula in the Schools: Survey of Large-Scale Assessment Program* (Lansing, Mich.: Michigan Department of Education, Fall 1989), p. 62.
11. National Endowment for the Arts, *Toward Civilization: A Report on Arts Education* (Washington, D.C., May 1988), p. 71.
12. Ibid., p. 75.
13. Thomas H. Fisher and Edward D. Roeber, *Assessment in the Arts and Foreign Languages*, a proposal prepared for the National Assessment Governing Board, Washington, D.C., October 1990.

14. John J. Cannell, *Nationally Normed Elementary Achievement Testing in America's Public Schools: How All Fifty States Are Above the National Average* (Daniels, W.V.: Friends of Education, 1987).

15. Theodor Rebarber, *Accountability in Education* (Denver, Colo.: National Conference of State Legislatures, July 1991).

16. Brent Wilson, *An Assessment Strategy for the Arts: Components of Comprehensive State and School District-Based Programs*, 1988, handout at the Arts Education Assessment Symposium sponsored by the Council of Chief State School Officers and the National Endowment for the Arts, December 4-6, 1991, Washington, D.C., p. 24.

17. Susan K. Vaughan, *Minnesota Statewide Assessments*, a report prepared for the "Arts Education Assessment Symposium," sponsored by the Council of Chief State School Officers and the National Endowment for the Arts, December 4-6, 1991, Washington, D.C.

18. Minnesota Department of Education, *Essential Learner Outcomes* (Saint Paul, Minn., December 1991).

19. Maryland State Board of Education, *Learning Outcomes for the Fine Arts* (Annapolis, Md., March 1991.

20. California Department of Education, *Summary of the Status of Arts Education Assessment in California* (Sacramento, Calif., December 1991).

PART IV

1. *Literacy in the Arts, An Imperative for New Jersey Schools*: (Trenton, N.J., October 1989) p. 32.

2. Ibid., p. 11.

3. Ibid., p. 12-14.

4. Ibid., p. 31.

5. Ibid., p. 32.

6. Ibid., p. 33.

7. Ibid., p. 35.

8. New Jersey State Department of Education, *Core Course Proficiencies: English (Language Arts)* (Trenton, N.J., n.d.), p. 7.

9. New Jersey State Department of Education, *Core Course Proficiencies: Social Studies Panel* (Trenton, N.J., n.d.), p. 8.

10. Jim Killackey, "HB 1017 Wins Arts Coalition's Endorsement," *Daily Oklahoman*, October 12, 1991, p. 5.

11. Oklahoma Department of Education, "Fine Arts Outcomes," *Oklahoma Educator* (January 1992), p. 7.

12. Sandy Garrett, "From the State Superintendent," *Administrative Focus* (Oklahoma City, Okla., September 16, 1991), p. 1.

13. Governor's Congress on the Arts and Humanities, "1995 State Action Plan for the Arts and Humanities: Recommendations: Education and Training Resolution," August 7, 1991, Oklahoma City, Okla., p. 1.

14. Ibid., p. 3-4.

15. South Carolina Business Education Committee, "An Evaluation of South Carolina's Education Improvement Efforts Five Years Later" (South Carolina, Winter 1988-89), p. 4.

16. South Carolina Department of Education, *What Is The Penny Buying For South Carolina?* (South Carolina, December 1, 1986), p. 24.

17. *Arts in Basic Curriculum Newsletter*, Winthrop College (Rock Hill, S.C., February 1990), p. 1.

18. Ibid., p. 28.

19. Peggy M. Siegel, *Education and Economic Growth: A Legislator's Guide* (Denver, Colo., National Conference of State Legislatures, 1988), p. 35.

PART V

1. "Forum: Arts Education and the K-12 Policy Complex," *Design for Arts in Education*, January 1988, p. 40.

2. National Endowment for the Arts (NEA), *Arts in Education Program: Arts in Schools Basic Education Grants 1990* (Washington, D.C., n.d.), p. 51.

3. Ronald Ross, "On the Need for New Partnerships on Arts Education," *Design for Arts in Education*, January 1991, p. 28.

4. National School Boards Association, *More Than Pumpkins in October*, p. 3.

5. Ibid.

6. Louis K. Stevens, *Planning to Make the Arts Basic*, A Report to the National Endowment for the Arts (Marion, Mass.: Arts Market Consulting, August 1991).

7. Ibid., p. 53.

8. NEA, *Arts in Education Program*, p. 50.

Ad Hoc Consortium of National Arts Education Associations. *Legislative and Policy Perspectives: Arts Education.* n.p., n.d. Available from the National Art Education Association, 1916 Association Drive, Reston, Va., 22091-1590.

American Alliance for Theater and Education, Music Educators National Conference, National Art Education Association. *National Arts Education Accord: A Statement on Arts Education to Governors and State Legislators.* Reston, Va., and Tempe, Ariz., 1991.

"Arts and Education: A Partnership Agenda." Report of a conference sponsored by the National Endowment for the Arts, Getty Center for Education in the Arts, National PTA, John F. Kennedy Center for the Performing Arts, Binney & Smith, Inc., March 1992, Washington, D.C.

Berk, Ellyn P. "What is a Family in the 1990s?" Statistics from Keynote Address, Third Annual Colorado K-16 Arts Education Summit, Colorado Department of Education, October 18, 1991.

Design for Arts in Education. Periodical published bimonthly by Heldref Publications, 1319 18th Street NW, Washington, D.C. 20036-1802.

Duke, Lelani Lattin. "What's Right With This Picture?" *State Legislatures* 17 (September 1991): 26-29.

Dreeszen, Craig. *Intersections: Community Arts and Education Collaborations.* Amherst, Mass.: University of Massachusetts at Amherst, Arts Extension Service, Division of Continuing Education, 1992.

Eisner, Elliot W. *The Role of Discipline-Based Art Education in America's Schools.* Los Angeles, Calif.: The Getty Center for Education in the Arts, n.d.

Fowler, Charles. *Can We Rescue The Arts For America's Children?* New York: ACA Books, 1988.

Fowler, Charles, and McMullan, Bernard. *Understanding How the Arts Contribute to Excellent Education.* Washington, D.C.: National Endowment for the Arts, 1991.

Gardner, Howard. *Frames of Mind: The Theory of Multiple Intelligences.* New York: Basic Books, 1983.

Goodwin, MacArthur; Crews, Edna; and Graybeal, Sheila. "Status of Arts Education Assessment in South Carolina." Photocopied. Columbia, S.C.: South Carolina Department of Education, November 1991.

Getty Center for Education in the Arts. From Snowbird I to Snowbird II: Final Report on the Getty Center Preserve Education Project. Los Angeles, Calif., 1990.

_____. *Arts for Life.* Videotape, 15 min. Los Angeles, Calif., 1990.

_____. *Beyond Creating: A Place for Art in America's Schools.* Los Angeles, Calif., April 1985.

Garcia, Eduardo, ed. *Arts Education in the United States: Highlights and Rankings of the States and Special Jurisdiction in the 1988-89 School Year.* Washington, D.C.: National Endowment for the Arts, December 1991.

Hanna, Judith Lynne. "Sponsored Activity That Supports Arts Education." Photocopied. Washington, D.C.: U.S. Department of Education, 1991.

_____. "Connections: Arts, Academics, and Productive Citizens." *Phi Delta Kappan* 73 (April 1992): 601-607.

_____. "Using The Arts as a Dropout Prevention Tool." *The Brown University Behavior and Child Development Newsletter* 7 (March 1991): 1-2.

Horn, Miriam. "Looking on a Renaissance: The Campaign to Revive Education in the Arts." *U.S. News and World Report,* March 30, 1992, 52-54.

Illinois State Board of Education. *Assessment Handbook: A Guide for Assessing Illinois Students.* Springfield, Ill., 1988.

Katz, Jonathan, ed. *Arts and Education Handbook: A Guide to Productive Collaborations.* Washington, D.C.: National Assembly of State Arts Agencies, 1988.

La Farge, Louisa, ed. *State Arts Agency Arts in Education Profiles.* 2nd edition. Washington, D.C.: National Endowment for the Arts, August 1991.

McLaughlin, John T., ed. *Toward a New Era in Arts Education.* New York, N.Y.: American Council for the Arts, 1988.

_____. *A Guide to National and State Arts Education Services.* New York, N.Y.: American Council for the Arts, 1987.

Maryland State Board of Education. "Fine Arts Assessment in Maryland." A description of the Maryland School Performance Program (Resolution No. 1989-53). Annapolis, Md.: December 12, 1989.

Music Educators National Conference. *Data on Music Education: A National Review of Statistics Describing Education in Music and the Other Arts.* Reston, Va., 1990.

Muszynski, Gary. "Arts Education Resource Center Survey." Paper prepared for the Missouri Arts Council. Photocopied. St. Louis, Mo., June 1989.

National Art Education Association. *Questions You Should Ask About The Art Programs In Your Schools. A Checklist Developed for Members of State Legislatures.* Reston, Va., n.d.

National Commission on Music Education. *Growing Up Complete: The Imperative for Music Education.* Reston, Va.: Music Educators National Conference, 1991.

National Endowment for the Arts. "Arts in Education Program: Arts in Schools Basic Education Grants, Fiscal Year 1990 Planning Grants." Photocopied. Washington, D.C., 1991.

_____. *Toward Civilization.* Washington, D.C., May 1988.

National School Boards Association. *More than Pumpkins in October: A Guide to Visual Literacy in the 21st Century,* Alexandria, Va., 1992.

New York Senate. Committee on Education and Select Committee on the Culture Industry. *Arts in Education.* Fact sheet. Albany, N.Y., 1988.

The State University of New York and the State Education Department. *A New Compact for Learning: Improving Public Elementary, Middle and Secondary Education Results in the 1990s.* New York, March 1991.

Pankratz, David B., and Morris, Valerie B. *The Future of the Arts: Public Policy and Arts Research.* New York, N.Y.: Praeger, 1990.

Price-Richard, Marilyn. *Art Education: Certification and Teacher.* Los Angeles, Calif., Getty Center for Education in the Arts. December 3, 1989.

Radich, Anthony. "Interorganizational Relationships in Arts Education Advocacy." Missouri Arts Council. Unpublished paper. St. Louis, Mo., March 1992.

Ross, Jerrold, and Berk, Ellyn. "Principal Research Findings 1987-1991." New York: National Arts Education Research Center, n.d.

Seidel, Kent. *Theater Education in United States High Schools: A Survey Report, Teaching Theater.* Cincinnati, Ohio: The Educational Theater Association, 1991.

Stevens, Louis K. *Planning to Make the Arts Basic. A Report to the National Endowment for the Arts.* Marion, Mass.: Arts Market Consulting, August 1991.

Williams, Harold. *The Language of Civilization: The Vital Role of Arts in Education.* New York, N.Y.: President's Committee on the Arts and Humanities, October 1991.

Wilson, Brent. *Art Education, Civilization and the 21st Century: A Researcher's Reflections on the National Endowment for the Arts Report to Congress.* Reston, Va.: National Art Education Association, n.d.

_____. *An Assessment Strategy for the Arts: Components of Comprehensive State and School District-Based Programs,* 1988. Handout at the Arts Education Assessment Symposium sponsored by the Council of Chief State School Officers and the National Endowment for the Arts, December 4-6, 1991, Washington, D.C.

Wolf, Dennie Palmer, and Pistone, Nancy. *Rethinking Assessment Through the Arts: Taking Full Measure.* New York, N.Y.: College Entrance Examination Board, 1991.

Laura L. Loyacono is the manager of the Arts, Tourism, and Cultural Resources Program of the National Conference of State Legislatures. In this capacity, she assists state legislators and their staffs in developing sound policy on a variety of issues, including tourism, historic preservation, and arts education. She also staffs the Arts and Tourism Committee of NCSL's Assembly on the Legislature and has written several NCSL publications including *Travel and Tourism: A Legislator's Guide*.

Before joining NCSL in 1987, Ms. Loyacono worked on the legislative staff of former Colorado Governor Richard D. Lamm. She attended Stephens College in Columbia, Missouri, where she earned her bachelor's degree in political science with a minor in theater arts and is working on her master's degree in political science at the University of Colorado, Denver.